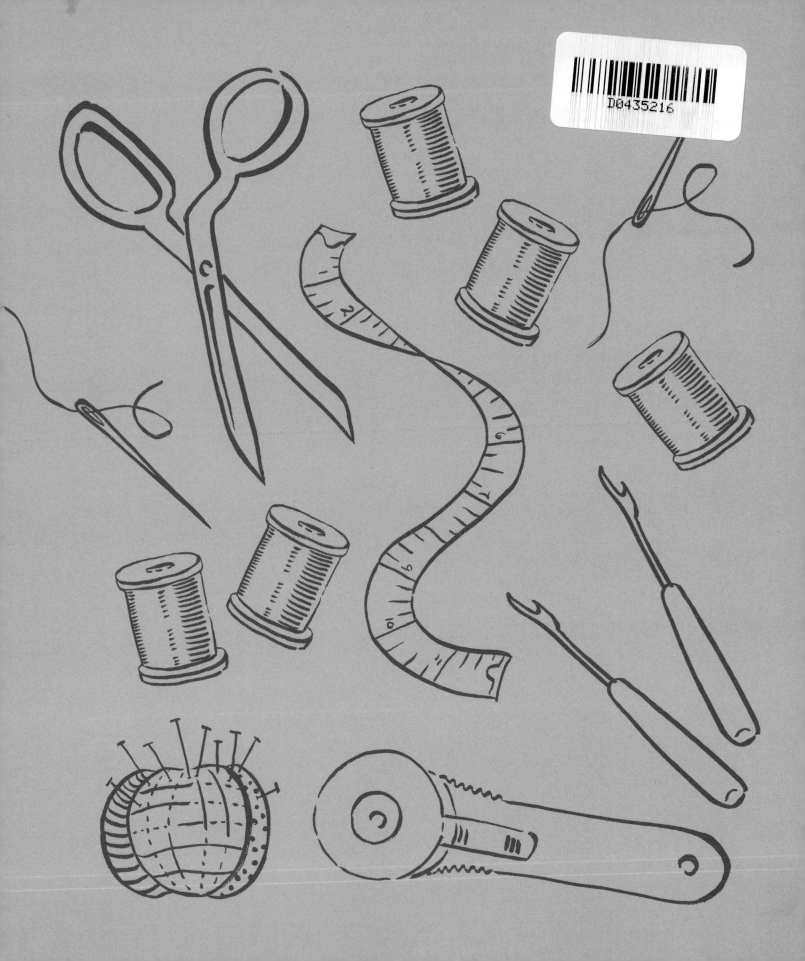

Sewing
for the first time®

Sewing
for the first time®

Mary Jo Hiney

Sterling Publishing Co., Inc.
New York
A Sterling / Chapelle Book

Chapelle:

Jo Packham, Owner

Cathy Sexton, Editor

Staff: Areta Bingham, Kass Burchett, Ray Cornia, Marilyn Goff, Karla Haberstich, Holly Hollingsworth, Susan Jorgensen, Barbara Milburn, Karmen Quinney, Caroll Shreeve, Cindy Stoeckl, Kim Taylor, Sara Toliver, Desirée Wybrow

Photographer: Kevin Dilley for Hazen Imaging, Inc.
Photo Stylist: Jill Dahlberg

Gallery Photography: Various professional photographers unknown by name, unless indicated.

If you have any questions or comments or would like information on specialty products featured in this book, please contact :

Chapelle, Ltd., Inc.
P.O. Box 9252, Ogden, UT 84409
(801) 621-2777 • (801) 621-2788 Fax
e-mail: chapelle@chapelleltd.com
website: www.chapelleltd.com

Library of Congress Cataloging-in-Publication Data Available

10 9 8 7 6 5 4 3

Published by Sterling Publishing Co., Inc.
387 Park Avenue South, New York, NY 10016
© 2002 by Mary Jo Hiney
Distributed in Canada by Sterling Publishing
c/o Canadian Manda Group, One Atlantic Avenue, Suite 105
Toronto, Ontario, Canada M6K 3E7
Distributed in Great Britain by Chrysalis Books
64 Brewery Road, London N7 9NT, England
Distributed in Australia by Capricorn Link (Australia) Pty. Ltd.
P.O. Box 704, Windsor, NSW 2756, Australia
Printed in China
All Rights Reserved

Sterling ISBN 0-8069-7283-1

For Mom
You taught me precise sewing skills
You inspired me with a love for fabric
You nurtured one of my favorite things about me
And a noble profession
Thanks, Mom

Table of Contents

Sewing for the first time

Introduction

The ability to sew is one of the best skills a person can possess. It is useful beyond imagination and can bring out personal or environmental individuality in one of its finest forms. If you get hooked on sewing, it will be a treasure to you that lasts a lifetime. In my opinion, when sewing, the most important commitment you can make to yourself is to finish what you start.

Are you one of those people who have trouble completing projects? You're not alone.

Many people get excited about the planning process and the hunting process; however, when it comes to the real work, they lose interest. Let me give you some helpful hints that I hope will inspire you.

First, if at all possible, prepare for yourself a small sewing area that will not have to be dismantled and reset every time you're in the mood to sew. The setting-up process, without a doubt, keeps you from beginning, let alone finishing your project. This small space can consist of a permanent place for your sewing machine to be set up, a place where an ironing board can be quickly placed, and a box to hold your work in progress and some tools. Perhaps you can use a room-divider screen to cover the space when not in use.

Second, separate your project into sections such as planning, shopping, cutting out, sewing parts, and finishing the details. Look at the sections of a project as goals to complete. Don't expect to start and finish your project in one sitting. This is not realistic. Set small goals and try to finish one section at that time.

Third, teach yourself how to find joy in the work itself. All of us have a time deficit and, as a society, we have been sucked into the fast-food mentality. Honestly speaking, do you really want to eat fast food exclusively? If you really want to enjoy sewing for life and do work you are proud of, you'll have to get past the fast-food mentality and buzz words like "quick and easy." Nothing worth putting your time into will be quick and easy. But, you can make quick work and easy work of a task by changing your attitude and receiving joy in the physical nature of a sewing project, or any project for that matter.

So, try to establish a permanent, but small, workspace. Divide your project into sections that you view as goals. Most importantly, learn how to enjoy the entire work process.

How to use this book

For the person who is sewing for the first time, this book provides a comprehensive guide to tools, notions, and techniques that encompass the sewing basics.

The intent of this book is to provide a starting point and to teach the basic skills. The more you sew, the more comfortable you will feel with fabric as your medium. Allow yourself a reasonable amount of time to complete your first project—remember, this is your first time.

You will soon discover that sewing techniques are easy to master simply by exposing yourself to the process and making it happen. Take pride in the abilities you are developing and know that you are playing a roll in continuing an ancient skill.

A glossary is provided at the back of this book to help you define words and/or terms that may not be familiar to you. It might be a good idea to read through the glossary as a starting point to help determine how often you might need to reference it.

Section 1 offers guidance for choosing a sewing machine and familiarizes you with the basic tools and notions you need to begin sewing. When first beginning to sew, you may be overwhelmed with the tools and notions that are available for sewing. Don't feel as though you must purchase every tool and notion that exists; however, it is important to familiarize yourself with your options.

Section 2 begins with the most basic technique—how to sew two surfaces together by stitching in a straight line. The second technique builds upon what you have already learned, adding the use of scissors for cutting out your project, then sewing a straight seam. Each subsequent technique continues in this manner, introducing a new technique and building on the previous one. If you decide to jump ahead out of sequence, you may find you have skipped a technique you now need to use. You can familiarize yourself with this needed technique by reading it through and practicing it on scrap fabric.

The last four techniques introduce you to the uses and different characteristics of unusual fabrics.

Section 3 provides a gallery of sewing designs done by artists and professionals in the field. These projects demonstrate the versatility that different types of fabric employ and hopefully will inspire you to create your own masterpieces.

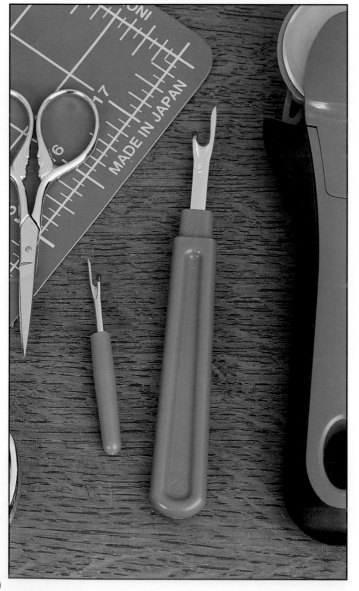

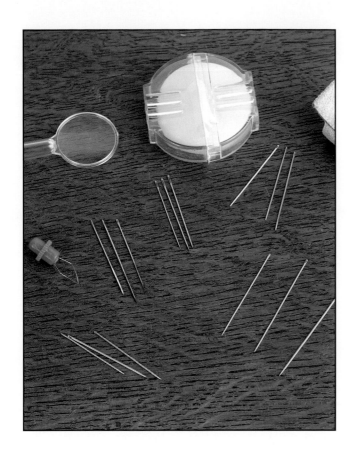

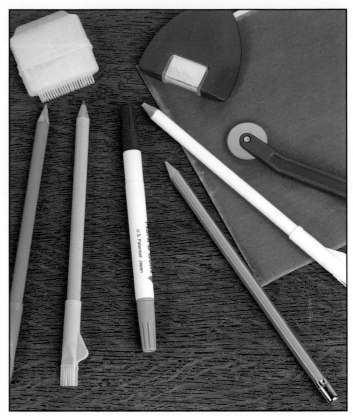

Section 1: *sewing basics*

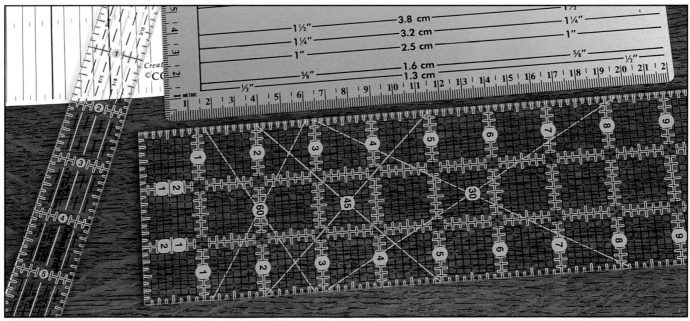

How do I choose a sewing machine?

Your sewing-machine retailer and consumer publications are the best sources of information when choosing a machine. Research your sewing machine options so you will make an informed decision. Sewing machines range from the basic utilitarian style to the sophisticated computer-programmed. Determine which of the machines you've researched will fill your present and projected needs.

Most sewing machine retailers offer classes with your purchase, enabling you to become completely familiar with all your sewing machine's capabilities. Another option is to purchase a used sewing machine.

If you already own a sewing machine, the sewing machine's manual is the best source of information for its operating use. Whether new, used, or already owned, thoroughly familiarize yourself with your sewing machine by spending time practicing with its features. Learning all about your sewing machine is a process in which you will spend many years, especially as you grow in skill.

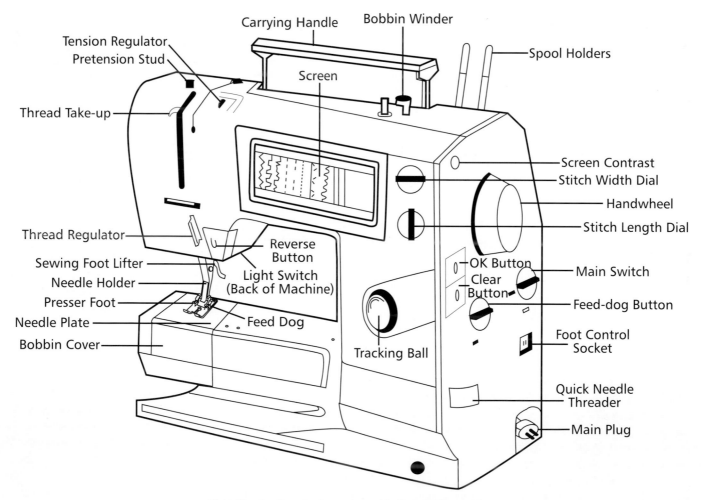

This illustration is for general information only.
The position of each sewing machine part could be different with each sewing machine manufacturer.

What types of threads should I use?

The basic all-purpose threads are the cotton-wrapped polyester core and the 100% polyester thread. These are the two types of threads that you will most often use for machine sewing. They are available in a wide color range. The cotton-wrapped polyester and the polyester threads have long-lasting durability.

When choosing thread, pick a shade that matches or is one shade darker than the fabric or fabric background. If your sewing machine is an older model, the polyester thread may not work as well as the cotton-wrapped polyester. One hundred percent cotton or silk threads are also basic thread types. These have an aesthetic quality but, because of their organic nature, will rot or deteriorate more rapidly over time.

For very specific uses, there are many other types of sewing machine threads available that you may desire to use as your skills increase, such as buttonhole twist and jeans topstitch threads, machine-embroidery threads, metallic and decorative threads, serger machine threads, machine-quilting threads, lingerie, invisible and fusible threads, and bobbin and basting threads.

What sewing machine needles should I use?

The type of sewing machine needles used are directed by the sewing machine manual, which is in conjunction with the type of fabric being sewn. Generally speaking, you can purchase a package that contains three or four different sized universal ballpoint needles to begin. Another great needle to have on hand is a "jeans" needle, especially if you are planning to hem denim fabric.

As you continue to learn and grow in skill, you will want to take advantage of the additional options available in sewing machine needles, options specifically intended to help do the sewing task better. These specialty needles include leather, imitation leather, topstitch, machine embroidery, twin or triple needles, hem-stitch, metallic, and spring needles.

How do I enlarge a pattern?

1. Make a photocopy of the pattern(s) you are working with from this book at your local copy center.

2. Enlarge the pattern(s) to the percentage(s) specified. It may be necessary to turn and copy the photocopy several times in order to enlarge the entire pattern.

3. When necessary, overlap and tape the enlarged pattern pieces together.

4. Keep in mind that you may alter the size of many of the projects in this book, simply by determining a new size and adjusting the amount of materials you need.

What measuring tools do I need?

1 Easy Hem Gauge

The easy hem gauge is used for measuring while pressing a hem in place.

2 Hem and Trim Measuring Guide

A hem and trim measuring guide is adhesive-backed and is made to be placed on your sewing machine.

3 Sewing Gauge

A sewing gauge with a movable slider is great for measuring and marking hems, buttonholes, tucks, pleats, scallops, and other sequences.

4 Tape Measure

A good fabric tape measure is a must! They are available in 60" lengths and 120" lengths, and have metric measurements on the reverse sides.

5 Transparent Grid-lined Ruler

A grid-lined ruler is a transparent straight-edged ruler with imprinted grid lines, available in an assortment of sizes. They are made from hard plastic and from flexible plastic, and are useful when using a rotary cutter.

Tips:

• *See-through rulers allow for checking the fabric grain line and markings.*

• *Special tools, called french curves, are made for altering curves on patterns.*

• *Placing undo stress on tape measures will cause them to lose accuracy. Replace them when they show wear.*

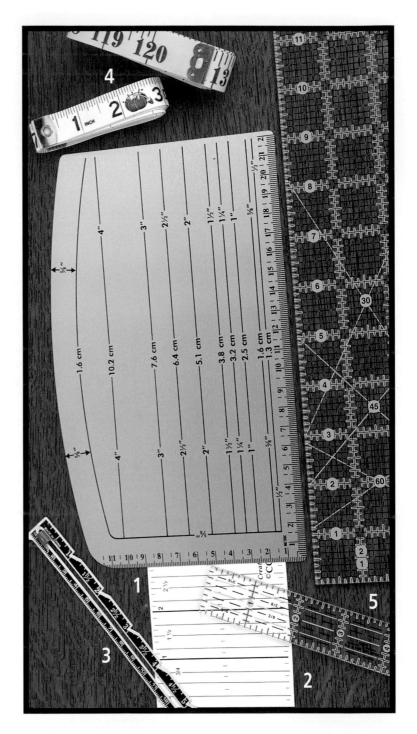

What fabric-marking tools do I need?

1 Dual-purpose Twin Marking Pen

We recommend a dual-purpose twin marking pen for the projects in this book. Keep in mind that the fabric(s) you have chosen may not be compatible with this type of marking pen. Therefore, a different marking tool also may be necessary. The word "twin" in the name indicates that this pen has two ends. One end contains blue ink that can be removed with a damp cloth. The other end contains purple disappearing ink that is both air and water soluble.

2 Dressmaker's Marking Pencil

A dressmaker's marking pencil is available with blue, pink, silver, and white lead. The marks can be removed with a damp cloth.

3 Tailor's Chalk or Chalk Wheel

Tailor's chalk or a chalk wheel are used for marking construction details and alterations on fabrics.

4 Tracing Wheel

A smooth tracing wheel is used to transfer pattern markings onto fabric and is used with wax-free tracing paper.

5 Wax-free Tracing Paper

Used with a tracing wheel or ballpoint pen, wax-free tracing paper is used to transfer pattern markings and design lines for embroidery and/or needlework.

What pinning tools do I need?

1 Pincushion/Magnetic Pin Holder

a. The classic tomato pincushion has a strawberry emery. The emery is used to sharpen and clean sewing needles. We recommend this pincushion for storing hand-sewing needles.

b. The magnetic pin holder is useful for holding straight pins as its magnetic field is generally large enough to successfully capture pins as they are "gently tossed" in the direction of the holder.

2 Straight Pins

Straight pins are essential for any sewing project. They come in different lengths. Pins with glass or plastic ball heads are great for basic sewing and are easy on the fingertips.

Nickel-plated steel pins are rust and corrosion resistant and will stick to magnets.

a. $1^{1}/_{16}$" ball-head pins are a nice length to work with for light- to medium-weight fabrics.

b. $1^{3}/_{8}$" ball-head pins, in extrafine, help out when working with delicate fabrics and machine piecing.

c. $1^{1}/_{4}$" flat-head pins, superfine sharp, will be useful when working with fine, delicate, or microfiber fabrics.

d. $1^{1}/_{2}$" ball-head pins with a fine shaft are ideal for quilting and home decorating projects.

e. $1^{3}/_{4}$" ball-head pins are considered extra long and are used when working with thick fabrics and multiple fabric layers.

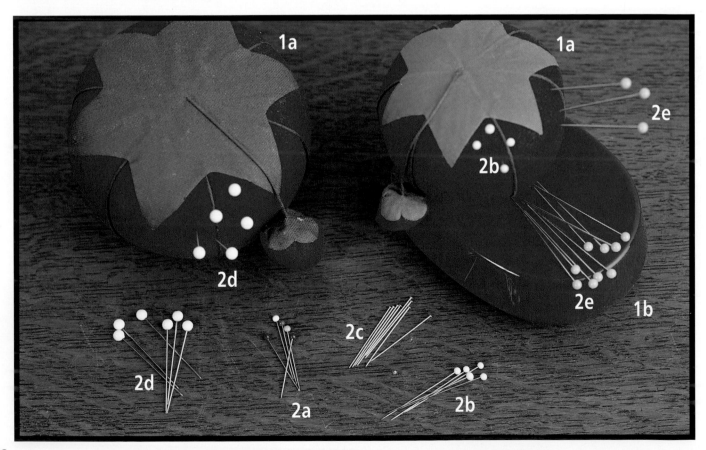

What cutting tools do I need?

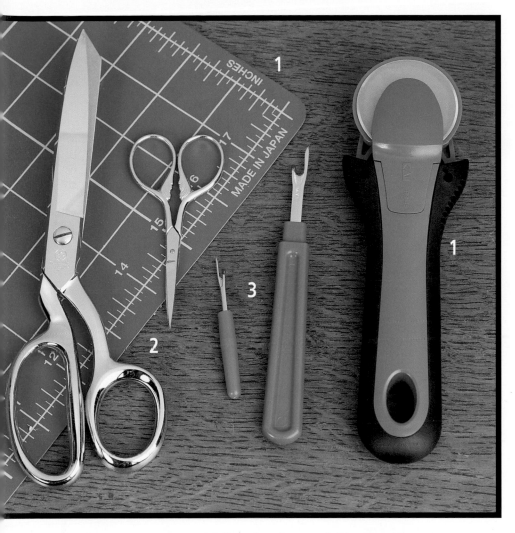

1   Rotary Cutter, Grid-lined Ruler, and Cutting Mat

The rotary cutter is a tool that looks and works like a pizza cutter, originally designed for quilt making. It has a round razor-type blade at the end of a handle, which is or can be covered when not in use. The blade is replaceable.

Though it takes some practice, many sewers prefer it over scissors, especially when making straight cuts. However, rotary cutters are not limited only to making straight cuts.

The rotary cutter must be used with a grid-lined ruler and a cutting mat. The cutting mat has a self-healing surface that absorbs the impact of the blade. You will want to choose one with precise grid markings. A large cutting mat can be kept out as an integral part of your sewing setup.

2   Scissors

When choosing your scissors, select pairs that have very sharp blades—this will add refinement to many aspects of sewing. Remember, if you purchase fine-quality pairs of scissors, they can last a lifetime!

The two pairs of scissors needed include a knife-edge bent scissor and a small knife-edge sewing scissor. The knife-edge bent scissors will be the most commonly used tool for cutting fabrics. They can be purchased in lightweight or featherweight, which will make cutting fabric easier for hands that may need a lighter handle. Scissor handles that are squeezed are also helpful for weak hands. The small knife-edge sewing scissors are used for trimming.

3   Seam Ripper

Mistakes happen—let a seam ripper be a useful tool for you. Use it to gently cut one or two stitches or an entire seam. Seam rippers are available in various sizes.

What pressing tools do I need?

1 Dressmaker's Ham

A dressmaker's ham is used for molding darts, curved seams, and sleeve caps.

2 Presscloth

A presscloth is an absolute must to protect fabrics when pressing.

3 Seam Roll

A seam roll is used for pressing long seams and narrow areas. It eliminates the seam allowance "ridge marks."

4 Sleeve Board

A sleeve board is used for pressing sleeves and small, hard-to-reach areas. This is a great investment!

5 Spray Bottle (not shown)

A spray bottle with water will be useful when pressing many fabrics. Use it with a presscloth.

6 Steam Iron and Ironing Board

A nonstick-coated steam iron plays an important part of every seam sewn. You will also need an ironing board that can be either full size or a smaller tabletop version.

Tips:

• *Always test a scrap of fabric for heat resistance. Too hot an iron can melt and/or scorch fibers.*

• *Use minimum pressure on the iron when pressing and press in the direction of the fabric grain. Lift the iron off the fabric to move to another section.*

• *Remove pins from fabric before pressing to prevent scratching the iron sole plate.*

What hand-sewing needles and tools do I need?

1 Ballpoint Needles

Ballpoint needles are used when working with stretch and knit fabrics.

2 Embroidery Needles

Embroidery needles are primarily the same as sharps, but they have longer eyes.

3 Leather Needles

Leather needles have triangular points for passing through leather without tearing it.

4 Milliner's Needles

Milliner's needles are long needles with small round eyes for basting and embroidery.

5 Sharps Needles

Sharps are basic hand-sewing needles that have sharp points.

6 Beeswax

Thread is run through the beeswax prior to hand-stitching to prevent tangling and to strengthen the thread.

7 Needle Threader

A needle threader is a tool used for threading needles quickly and easily. For added convenience, needle threaders are also available with a magnifier attached.

8 Thimble

A thimble is used to protect your fingertips from painful needle pricks. It takes practice and determination to use.

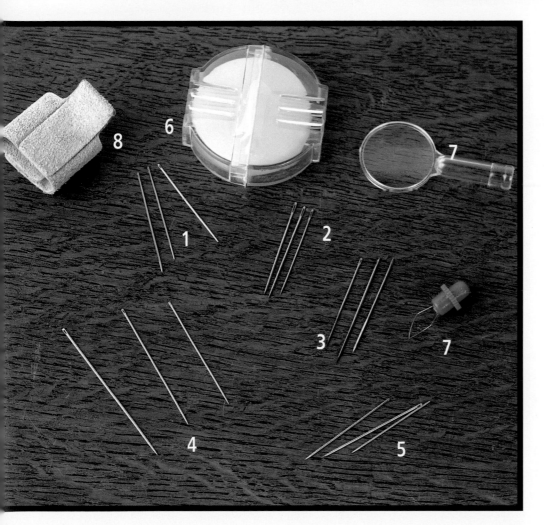

Tips:

• *Change needles often. A bent or dull needle can ruin fabric.*

• *Needles come in number scales. The larger the number, the shorter and thinner the needle.*

What additional sewing aids do I need?

1 Adhesive Hem Tape

Adhesive hem tape comes on a roll and is great for quick hems.

2 Ballpoint Bodkin

A ballpoint bodkin is used to insert ribbon or elastic in a casing, turn bias tubing, or weave ribbon.

3 Elastic Guide

An elastic guide keeps elastic and ribbon from twisting while inserting into casings.

4 Fray Preventative

This liquid edge sealant prevents fabric and ribbon from fraying.

5 Iron Cleaner

A good iron cleaner is imperative to the life of your iron. It removes starches and fusible interfacing from the surface of your iron.

6 Lint Brush

A lint brush is used for cleaning your sewing machine.

7 Loop Turner

A loop turner is used to turn bias tubing.

8 Point Turner

A point turner aids in pushing out corners once the project is turned "right side out."

9 Sewing/Craft Glue Stick

A sewing/craft glue stick is used for basting and positioning hems, zippers, trims, and appliqués.

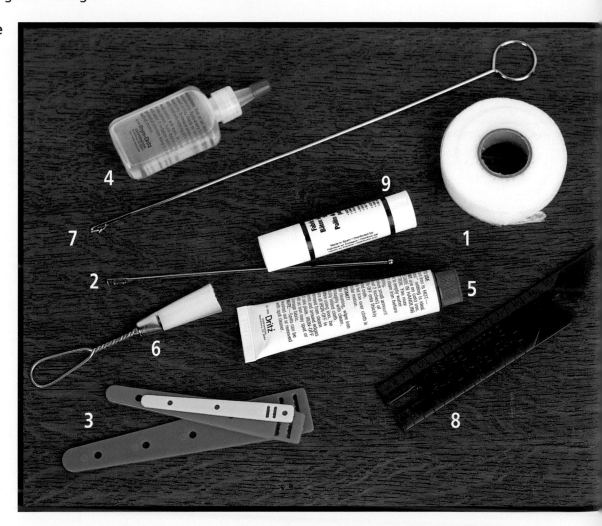

What notions do I need?

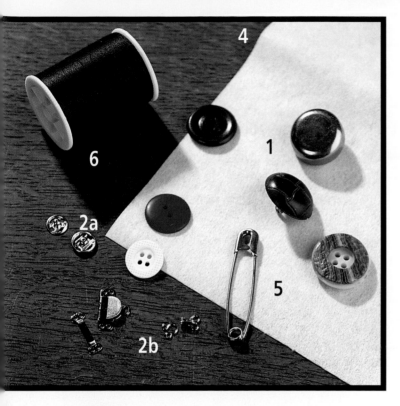

1 Buttons

The right button is the "icing on the cake" for a well-loved project. Take extra care and time when selecting buttons for your projects. You can choose a button with holes or a button with a shank on the back.

2 Closures

a. Sew-on snaps are used for closing a garment or accessory. They are available in nickel or black enamel-coated metal in a variety of sizes.

b. Hooks and eyes also are used as closures and are available in a variety of brass, nickel, and black enamel-coated metal styles and sizes.

3 Elastic (not shown)

Elastic is a narrow braid made from rubber or stretchable fiber and used primarily in garment construction for very specific purposes.

4 Interfacing

An interfacing is used to add an appropriate amount of shaping or stiffness to a garment or accessory detail by adding body or stability to an edge, neckline, cuff, collar, pocket, buttonhole, or other construction detail without interferring with the natural drape of the fabric. Its type of application, being either a sew-in type or a fusible type, characterizes an interfacing. It should never be heavier in weight than the outer fabric.

Fusible interfacings, available as woven, knit, or nonwoven, are coated on one side with an adhesive. These are adhered on the wrong side of the outer fabric with iron heat, steam, and pressure. Sometimes the adhesive has an undesirable result, such as staining the outer fabric or causing the outer fabric to not drape freely. To avoid this, test the interfacing on the intended fabric prior to use.

Sew-in interfacings are available as either woven or nonwoven and are stitched by hand or machine to your garment or accessory.

All interfacings are available in a variety of weights and degrees of crispness. Some basic fabrics are also used as an interfacing, such as organza, cotton batiste, and cotton sheeting. Some sewers prefer to use the outer fabric as self-interfacing.

5 Safety Pin

A large safety pin can be a useful tool. Most often, it is used for turning "handles" or "straps" right side out. To do this, place the safety pin at one end of the handle or strap, manipulating it within the handle, and finally drawing the fabric through the length of the handle.

6 Threads (see page 13)

7 Zippers (not shown)

The conventional zipper is available with nylon or metal teeth and ranges in lengths from 8" to 24". A wide variety of colors is available.

How do I use a rotary cutter?

1. Fold the fabric you are using in half, right sides together, aligning the selvage edges as shown below.

Note: Folding the fabric is the process used for doubling the layers. This does not necessarily mean the pattern(s) will be "cut" on the fold. The dimensions used on individual projects will represent the actual size of the individual pieces cut from the appropriate fabrics.

Tips:

• *Practice using a rotary cutter and ruler on scrap fabric of the same weight as your project before cutting the actual piece out.*

• *Arrange the cutting table so you can move around all sides to cut from different angles.*

• *Cut groups of pattern pieces or fabrics so they can be turned around if you cannot get to all sides of the cutting table.*

• *Make certain the fabric is laid out and folded correctly before beginning to cut.*

2. Place the folded fabric on the cutting mat so the folded edge is parallel to the bottom edge of the mat (toward you) as shown below.

Align the folded edge with a horizontal grid line on the cutting mat and the right edge with a vertical grid line on the cutting mat. The folded edge can line up perfectly with a horizontal grid line, but the vertical edge probably will not. The purpose of this is to cut the vertical edge, which is the crosswise grain of the fabric, straight and square.

3. Align a horizontal mark on the grid-lined ruler with the folded edge of the fabric and a horizontal line on the cutting mat. Simultaneously align the vertical edge of the grid-lined ruler with the right vertical edge of the fabric and a vertical line on the cutting mat as shown below.

4. Holding the ruler firmly in place with one hand and the rotary cutter firmly with the other hand, trim away the vertical edge of the fabric by placing the blade of the rotary against the outer edge of the ruler and rolling, as with a pizza cutter, as shown below. Make certain to keep fingertips away from the blade.

Always cut perpendicular to your body, and away from you, as it is the safest direction and the one in which you will have the most control.

Reposition the ruler as necessary for the width of the fabric being cut.

Section 2:
basic techniques

How do I sew two surfaces together by stitching in a straight line?

All sewing machines naturally stitch in a forward direction using a very basic straight stitch. You control the fabric as it is fed through the machine.

What You Will Need:

To make each embellished hand towel:

- Basic tools and supplies, see pages 12–21
- Terry cloth hand towel
- Ribbon, 1"- to 2"-wide (¹/₂ yard)

Embellished Hand Towels

Here's How:

Sewing the Ribbon on the Hand Towels

1. Place the lengths of ribbon widthwise across the band portions of the towels.

2. Folding each end of the ribbon under, pin the ribbon in place with straight pins placed vertically at 2" intervals along both selvage edges of the ribbon as shown in Diagram A below.

3. Refer to the Glossary: Backstitch on page 108. Backstitch to lock the stitches.

Refer to the Glossary: Stitch on page 108. Stitch the entire length of the ribbon as close to its selvage edges as possible as shown in Diagram B below. Remove the pins as you stitch.

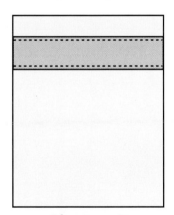

Diagram B

Finishing the Hand Towels

1. Press the ribbon from the wrong sides of the towels.

Note: Pressing is a key factor to any well-made project. Keep in mind that there are different ways stitched surfaces may need to be pressed.

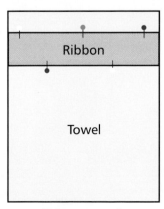

Diagram A

Design Tips:

• Use thread that matches the color of the ribbon for the "upper thread" and thread that matches the color of the towel for the "bobbin thread."

• When using narrow ribbon, it may be necessary to stitch down the center of the ribbon instead of along each of the selvage edges.

2
technique

What You Will Need:

To make one
12" x 12" pillow:

- Basic tools and supplies, see pages 12–21
- Cotton/linen blend home decorator's fabric, toile pattern, 54"-wide ($^1/_2$ yard) for Front and Back
- Pillow form, 12"-square

Design Tip:

• *When square or rectangular pieces of fabric are sewn into a pillow, the corners will appear as though they were purposely exaggerated. To avoid this, gradually taper the corners by $^1/_2$" while sewing.*

How do I cut fabric and sew a straight seam?

A straight cut is a simple task to accomplish with the right tools: either a sharp pair of scissors or a rotary cutter, a fabric-marking pen or pencil, and a good ruler. A straight seam is also easy to accomplish when using the guide provided on your sewing machine.

Basic Pillow

Here's How:

Cutting the Fabric

1. Refer to How do I use a rotary cutter? on pages 22–23. Cut the fabric for the Front and the Back of the pillow 13" square as shown in Diagram A below.

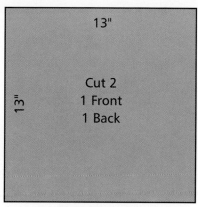

Diagram A

Sewing the Side Seams

1. Place the Front over the Back, right sides together, aligning each side.

2. Beginning near one of the corners, pin the two layers together with straight pins placed vertically at 2" intervals around the entire pillow as shown in Diagram B below.

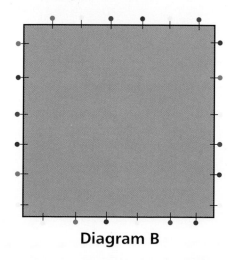

Diagram B

3. Refer to the Glossary: Backstitch on page 108. Backstitch to lock the stitches.

Refer to the Glossary: Stitch on page 108. Stitch the seam line, using a 1/2" seam allowance.

Begin by placing the sewing machine needle in the fabric approximately 1 1/2" from one of the corners and 1/2" from the cut edge of the fabric as shown in Diagram C below.

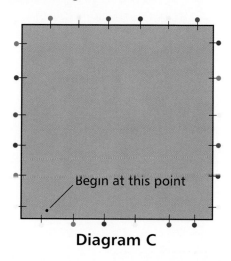

Begin at this point

Diagram C

Stitch for 1" and stop while the needle is in the downward position. Pivot the fabric layers to the next side and continue stitching. Stop 1/2" short of the next corner as shown in Diagram D below, again making certain the needle is in the downward position. Remove the pins as you stitch.

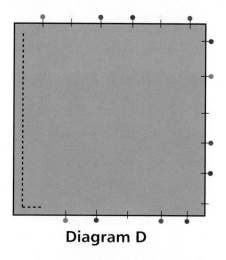

Diagram D

Repeat until three of the sides have been sewn. End by stitching the last side 1" as shown in Diagram E below.

Diagram E

Finishing the Pillow

1. Using scissors, clip the bulk from each corner as shown in Diagrams F and G below.

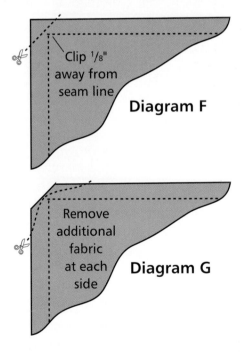

Clip ⅛" away from seam line

Diagram F

Remove additional fabric at each side

Diagram G

2. Edge-press the seam lines and seam allowances on one side of the fabric. To do this, fold over the top layer of the seam allowances as shown in Diagram H at left and press.

Repeat until all four of the sides have been edge-pressed.

Note: Edge-pressing will help expose the seam line when the fabric is turned right side out. Unlike pressing a seam allowance open, in this case only one side of the seam allowance has been pressed open. This method of pressing is used when it is not possible to press a seam allowance open.

3. Press the seam allowance under at the pillow cover opening.

4. Turn the pillow cover right side out through the opening along the bottom. To do this, place your hand through the seam opening and push out the corners from the inside. Using a point turner, accentuate each corner.

5. Fold the pillow form in half and insert it into the pillow cover through the opening.

Adjust the pillow form so the corners align with the corners of the pillow cover.

6. Pin the opening closed and stitch the entire length of the opening as close to the edges as possible as shown in Diagram I below.

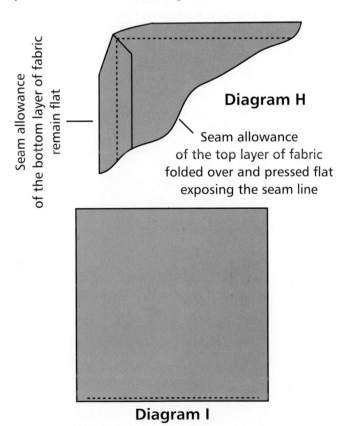

Seam allowance of the bottom layer of fabric remain flat

Diagram H

Seam allowance of the top layer of fabric folded over and pressed flat exposing the seam line

Diagram I

How do I use topstitching in a functional rather than a decorative manner?

Topstitching can be found on many garments and accessories. Sometimes it is used decoratively—other times it is used functionally to help control the fabric by stabilizing the layers.

What You Will Need:

To make one
13" x 52" table runner:

- Basic tools and supplies,
  see pages 12–21
- Chenille tapestry fabric,
  floral pattern,
  54"-wide (¹/₂ yard)
  for Top
- Satin home decorator's
  fabric, striped pattern,
  54"-wide (¹/₂ yard)
  for Back

Reversible Table Runner

Here's How:

Cutting the Fabrics

1. Fold the chenille fabric for the Top in half, right sides together, aligning selvage edges as shown in Diagram A below.

Place the folded fabric, which measures 18" wide x 27" long, on a cutting mat, aligning the folded edge with a horizontal grid line.

2. Refer to How do I use a rotary cutter? on pages 22–23. Trim the right edge of the fabric so it is straight, trimming off as little as necessary to make a clean cut.

3. Measure 13" from the trimmed edge of the fabric and mark, using a fabric-marking pen or pencil at randomly spaced intervals as shown in Diagram B below.

Note: If using a fabric that is incompatible with the use of a fabric-marking pen or pencil, mark the measurement with a straight pin placed vertically where the mark should be.

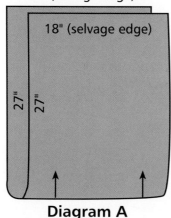

18" (selvage edge)

18" (selvage edge)

27"   27"

Diagram A

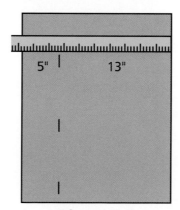

5"   13"

Diagram B

4. Repeat Step 2 on page 31, leaving approximately 5" of scrap fabric.

5. Repeat Step 1 on page 31 with the satin fabric for the Back.

6. Repeat Step 2.

7. Repeat Step 3 on page 31, measuring 15" from the trimmed edge of the fabric.

8. Repeat Step 2, leaving approximately 3" of scrap fabric.

Note: Because fabric widths are not universal, place both pieces of fabric together, aligning one selvage and one cut edge. Trim the difference from the necessary fabric so both fabrics are the exact length (approximately 54").

Sewing the Long Edges

1. Place the Top over the Back, right sides together, aligning one long edge.

2. Beginning at the top of one long edge, pin the two layers together with straight pins placed vertically at 9" intervals.

Note: Make certain to align the fabrics at the very top edges and the very bottom edges of the seam line.

3. Refer to the Glossary: Backstitch on page 108. Backstitch to lock the stitches.

Refer to the Glossary: Stitch on page 108. Stitch the seam line, using a 3/8" seam allowance as shown at right. Remove the pins as you stitch.

4. Press the seam line flat to blend the stitches into the fabric as shown at right.

Press the seam allowance toward the Back.

5. Repeat Steps 1–4 above, sewing the remaining long edge. However, in this seam line, an opening must be left for turning the table runner right side out. To do this, discontinue the stitching for a 4" space near the center.

Sewing the Short Edges

Note: Right sides should still be together.

1. Position the fabrics so the Top is centered over the Back. The Back will extend 1/2" over each side of the Top.

2. Pin and stitch one short edge, using a 1/2" seam allowance.

3. Repeat Step 2 above, sewing the remaining short edge.

Finishing the Table Runner

1. Refer to Technique 2: Finishing the Pillow, Step 1 on page 30. Clip the bulk from each corner as shown below.

2. Refer to Technique 2: Finishing the Pillow, Step 2 on page 30. Edge-press the end seams with Back side down as shown below.

3. Refer to Technique 2: Finishing the Pillow, Step 4 on page 30. Turn the table runner right side out through the opening along the side seam as shown below.

Note: If necessary, a straight pin can be used to gently capture and pull the fabric from the outside to help bring the corner out. Care must be taken not to pull the fabric threads.

4. Adjust the fabric so there is a 1/2" border from the Back along the side edges of the Top and press as shown below.

5. Because the seam allowance is pressed toward the Back, the Top at the seam line naturally slips underneath the 1/2" border at the seam line.

Thread the hand-sewing needle with a length of thread and knot the thread ends together.

6. Refer to the Glossary: Slip stitch on page 107. Slip-stitch the opening closed as shown below. To do this, slip the needle into the chenille fabric at one end of opening at its folded edge, hiding the knot within the fold. Pick up a small amount of satin fabric directly opposite the needle exit point and along the seam line. Slip the needle back into the folded edge and pull the thread through. Continue in this manner, making stitches 1/4" apart.

7. Refer to the Glossary: Topstitch on page 108. To help the table runner lie flat, topstitch along the short edges and press.

8. Refer to the Glossary: Stitch in the ditch on page 108. To further secure the layers of fabric, stitch in the ditch between the Top and Back along the long edges as shown below and press. To do this, press the seam to one side—in this case, toward the lining. Position the table runner, right side up, on the sewing machine. Pass the needle down into the seam line between the two pieces of fabric. Holding the seam flat, stitch on the seam line the entire length of the seam, through all layers of fabric. Press after stitching and repeat for the other side.

Note: Stitch in the ditch is a technique used to flatten a seam line and secure it to a backing fabric. It also keeps the unseamed edge from rolling. This method can also be used on a seam that has been pressed open.

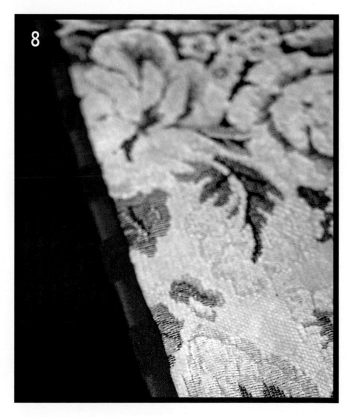

How do I make a basic pillowcase?

Stitched with straight seams and a simple hem, a basic pillowcase is one of the easiest pieces to create. With only a little extra effort, a complementary fabric band can be added to give your piece a truly sophisticated designer look.

What You Will Need:

To make each standard-sized (20" x 32") pillowcase:

- Basic tools and supplies, see pages 12–21
- Cotton fabric, 44" wide ($^3/_8$ yard) for Band
- Cotton fabric, 44"-wide ($^7/_8$ yard) for Body
- Cotton fabric, 44" wide ($^1/_8$ yard) for Strip at top of Band

Basic Pillowcase

Here's How:

Cutting the Fabrics

1. Refer to How do I use a rotary cutter? on pages 22–23. Cut the fabric for each Body 28" wide x 41" long as shown in Diagram A below.

Cut the fabric for each Band 11" wide x 41" long as shown in Diagram B below.

Cut the fabric for each Strip 1½" wide x 41" long as shown in Diagram C below.

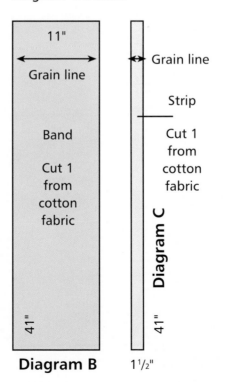

28"

← Grain line →

Body

Cut 1 from cotton fabric

41"

Diagram A

11"

← Grain line →

Band

Cut 1 from cotton fabric

41"

Diagram B

Grain line

Strip

Cut 1 from cotton fabric

Diagram C

41"

1½"

Sewing the Band to the Body

1. Fold the Strip in half, wrong sides together, aligning the long edges and press.

2. Pin the folded Strip to one long edge of the right side of the Body with straight pins placed vertically, aligning the cut edges.

3. Refer to the Glossary: Machine baste stitch on page 108. Baste-stitch in place, using a $^3/_8$" seam allowance as shown below. Remove the pins as you stitch.

Note: The baste stitch makes the Strip manage-able when the Band is sewn to the Body. When the Band is stitched in place with a wider seam allowance, the basting stitches will not show.

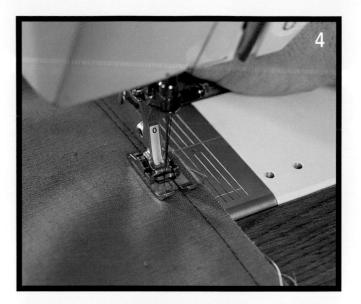

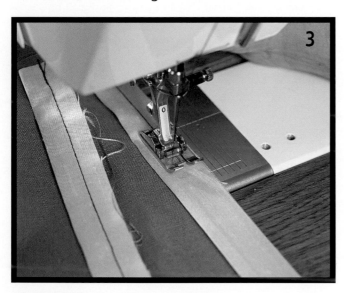

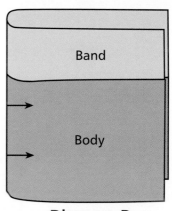

4. Refer to the Glossary: Backstitch on page 108. Backstitch to lock the stitches.

Refer to the Glossary: Stitch on page 108. Pin and stitch one long edge of the Band to the Body with Strip, right sides together, using a $^1/_2$" seam allowance as shown at top right.

5. Trim the seam allowance to $^1/_4$". Press the seam allowance toward the Band as shown at center right.

Matching the Crossing Seams

1. Fold the pillowcase in half, right sides together, aligning the short edges as shown in Diagram D at right.

Diagram D

2. To perfectly match the seam lines, push a straight pin into the upper layer of fabric (wrong side of seam line is facing you) directly through the seam line at the seam allowance.

Move the fabric layers together and complete the pinning motion by pushing the pin directly through the aligning seam line as shown below.

3. To ensure the match is perfect, pin the fabric layers together on either side of the first pin with $1/8$" space between pins as shown below.

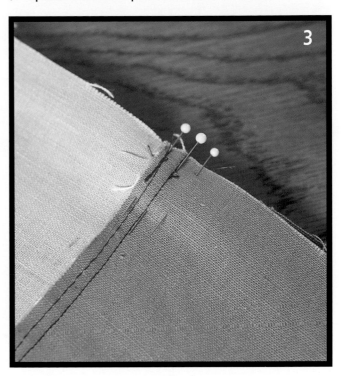

4. Finish pinning the rest of the edge, aligning the fabric at the top and bottom ends.

5. Stitch the seam line, using a $1/2$" seam allowance.

<table>
<tr><td>5
technique</td><td></td></tr>
</table>

How do I choose a seam and hem finish for my basic pillowcase?

There are several simple alternatives with which to finish the seams and hems of your basic pillowcase. The seam and hem finishes are interchangeable and easily applied to give your piece the unique tailored detail you desire.

Pillowcase Option 1:
Seam Finish: Pressed Open
Hem Finish: Machine-hemming

The model featured here was made from yellow floral-print and peach with yellow polka-dot preshrunk cotton fabrics with a contrasting fabric strip at the band.

Note: It is now time to choose which seam and hem finishes you will use. For other seam and hem finishing options, see pages 42–47.

Finishing the Seam

1. For a basic pillowcase, finish the seam by pressing the seam allowance open as shown below.

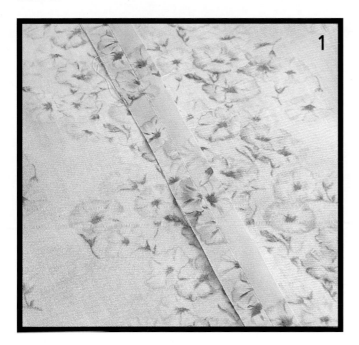

Hemming the Pillowcase
Along the Open End

1. Hem the pillowcase by machine. To do this, turn the pillowcase wrong side out. Press the bottom edge of the Band under ½" to the wrong side of the fabric.

Fold and press the Band in half, wrong sides together, aligning the pressed-under edge with the Band seam line.

Pin in place with straight pins placed vertically.

Note: Since this will be a machine-sewn hem, stitched from the right side, the pressed-under edge should lay approximately ⅛" over the Band/Body seam line. This will ensure that the pressed-under edge will be completely caught when stitched.

2. Refer to the Glossary: Backstitch on page 108. Backstitch to lock the stitches.

Refer to the Glossary: Stitch on page 108. Working from the right side of the pillowcase, stitch the hem by stitching just to the left of the Band/Body seam line as shown below and press. Remove the pins as you stitch.

Note: If a decorative hem is preferred, this is a great time to experiment on scrap fabric with some machine-embroidery stitches and rayon machine-embroidery thread. When comfortable, machine-embroider the hem in place.

Sewing the Closed End

1. With right sides together, pin and stitch the bottom edge, using a ½" seam allowance, having the seam at one side.

2. Refer to Technique 2: Finishing the Pillow, Step 1 on page 30. Clip the bulk from each corner.

3. Refer to Technique 2: Finishing the Pillow, Step 2 on page 30. Edge-press the end seam allowance open.

4. Turn the pillowcase right side out. Push out the corners from the inside. Using a point turner, accentuate each corner and press.

Pillowcase Option 2:
Seam Finish: Zigzag-stitched
Hem Finish: Hand-hemming

The model featured here was made from gray-print preshrunk cotton and white linen fabrics with a contrasting fabric strip at the band.

Finishing the Seam

1. For this pillowcase, cut the fabrics, sew the Band to the Body, and match the crossing seams as instructed on pages 38–39.

2. Trim the seam allowance to ¼".

3. Refer to the Glossary: Zigzag stitch on page 108. Zigzag-stitch along the edge of the seam allowance as shown below.

4. Press the seam allowance toward one side, which will designate that side as the back.

Hemming the Pillowcase Along the Open End

1. Hem the pillowcase by hand. To do this, turn the pillowcase wrong side out. Press the bottom edge of the Band under ½" to the wrong side of the fabric.

Fold and press the Band in half, wrong sides together, aligning the pressed-under edge with the Band seam line.

Pin in place with straight pins placed vertically.

2. Thread the hand-sewing needle with a length of thread and knot the ends together. Refer to the Glossary: Slip stitch on page 107. Slip-stitch the hem in place, working from the inside of the pillowcase. To do this, slip the needle into the

folded edge of the Band fabric at the side seam line, hiding the knot within the fold. Pick up a small amount of Body fabric directly opposite the needle exit point and along the seam line. Slip the needle back into the folded edge and pull the thread through. Continue in this manner, making stitches ¼" apart. Remove the pins as you stitch.

Sewing the Closed End

1. Refer to the Glossary: Backstitch on page 108. Backstitch to lock the stitches.

Refer to the Glossary: Stitch on page 108. With right sides together, pin and stitch the bottom edge, using a ½" seam allowance, having the seam at one side.

2. Refer to Technique 2: Finishing the Pillow, Step 1 on page 30. Clip the bulk from each corner.

3. Zigzag-stitch the seam allowance as shown below.

4. Turn the pillowcase right side out. Push out the corners from the inside. Using a point turner, accentuate each corner and press.

Pillowcase Option 3:
Seam Finish: French Seam
Hem Finish: Narrow Machine-hemming

The model featured here was made from embroidered organza and dotted Swiss fabrics.

Finishing the Seam

1. For this pillowcase, cut the Body 28" wide x 41" long and the Band 6" wide x 41" long.

Pin one long edge of the Band to the Body edge with straight pins placed vertically, wrong sides together.

2. Refer to the Glossary: Backstitch on page 108. Backstitch to lock the stitches.

Refer to the Glossary: Stitch on page 108. To make the French seam, stitch the seam line, using a ¹/₄" seam allowance as shown below. Remove the pins as you stitch.

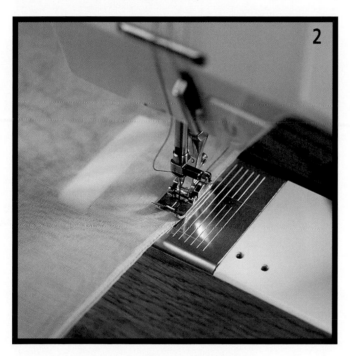

3. Trim the seam allowance to ¹/₈".

4. Press the seam allowance toward the organza fabric. Fold the fabric along the seam line, right sides together, and press.

Pin and stitch, using a ¹/₄" seam allowance. Press the seam allowance toward the organza.

5. Repeat Matching the Crossing Seams: Steps 1–4 on pages 38–39, beginning with wrong sides together and sewing a French seam on the side as in Steps 2–4 above.

6. Press the seam allowance toward one side, which will designate that side as the back.

Hemming the Pillowcase Along the Open End

1. Hem the pillowcase with a narrow machine-sewn hem. To do this, fold the raw edge of the dotted swiss fabric over ¹/₄" to the wrong side. Fold over again and stitch along the outside edge of the fold as shown below, forming a ¹/₄"-wide hem and press.

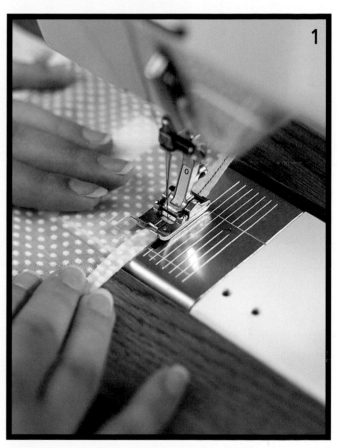

Sewing the Closed End

1. Sew a French seam across the bottom as in Steps 2–4 at left.

2. Turn the pillowcase right side out. Push out the corners from the inside. Using a point turner, accentuate each corner and press.

Pillowcase Option 4:
Seam Finish: Flat-felled Seam
Hem Finish: Decorative Machine-hemming

The model featured here was made from pink floral-print preshrunk cotton and dotted Swiss fabrics.

Finishing the Seam

1. For this pillowcase, cut the Body 33" wide x 41" long and the Band 6" wide x 41" long.

Pin the Body short edges with straight pins placed vertically, wrong sides together.

2. Refer to the Glossary: Backstitch on page 108. Backstitch to lock the stitches.

Refer to the Glossary: Stitch on page 108. To make the flat-felled seam, stitch the short edges together, using a $1/2$" seam allowance. Remove the pins as you stitch.

3. Trim one layer of the seam allowance to $1/4$".

4. Press the seam allowance toward one side. Turn the edge of the longer seam allowance under $1/4$" and place it over the trimmed seam allowance.

Stitch close to the folded edge and press as shown below.

5. Fold the Band in half, right sides together, aligning the short edges.

Stitch the short edges, using a $1/2$" seam allowance.

6. Press the seam allowance open.

7. Pin the right side of one edge of the Band to the wrong side of one edge of the Body.

Stitch around the edges, using a $1/2$" seam allowance.

8. Trim the seam allowance to $1/4$".

9. Press the seam allowance toward the Band, then turn the Band to the right side. Press the Band in place over the fabric as shown below.

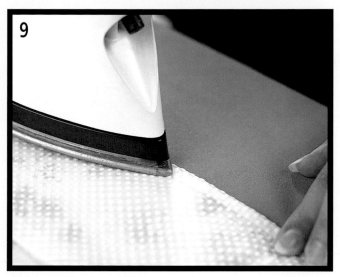

Hemming the Pillowcase Along the Open End

1. Hem the pillowcase with a machine-top-stitched hem. To do this, turn the raw edge of the Band under $1/2$" to the wrong side and press.

Pin the Band over the Body and stitch in place on the right side of the fabric, stitching close to the turned-under edge.

Sewing the Closed End

1. With right sides together, pin and stitch the bottom edge, using a $1/2$" seam allowance, having the seam at one side.

2. Refer to Technique 2: Finishing the Pillow, Step 1 on page 30. Clip the bulk from each corner.

3. Refer to the Glossary: Zigzag stitch on page 108. Zigzag-stitch the seam allowance.

4. Turn the pillowcase right side out. Push out the corners from the inside. Using a point turner, accentuate each corner and press.

How do I finish the inside of a project with a lining?

Lining is a duplicate application of identical or similar pattern pieces for a garment or accessory. Linings can be made from utilitarian or decorative fabrics. The assembled pieces are made with wrong sides facing, thus creating a perfect inner appearance and built-in protection.

What You Will Need:

To make one lined handbag:

- Basic tools and supplies, see pages 12–21
- Vintage fabric, floral pattern, 54"-wide ($^3/_4$ yard) for Handbag
- Satin home decorator's fabric, striped pattern, 54"-wide ($^3/_4$ yard) for Lining
- Buttons, (2) $1^1/_4$"

Lined Handbag

Here's How:

Preparing the Patterns

1. Enlarge the Sides and Handles Patterns on page 54 to 250%. Cut out the patterns.

Laying Out the Patterns

1. Fold the vintage fabric in half, right sides together, aligning selvage edges.

Note: Generally, fabric is folded in half, right sides together, aligning selvage edges prior to the layout of the pattern pieces. However, the main objective is to use the fabric as economically as possible, so this general rule may not always apply.

2. Position the patterns on the folded vintage fabric, aligning the grain line pattern markings with the selvage edges, leaving enough fabric for the Front and the Back.

On the remaining area of the fabric, measure and mark one 16" x 20$^1/_2$" rectangular piece on the vintage fabric, using a fabric-marking pen or pencil, for the Front and the Back of the handbag as shown in Diagram A at right.

3. Beginning with the pattern grain lines, pin the pattern pieces to the vintage fabric, measuring from the pattern grain line to the selvage edge to make certain the pieces are straight and equally distanced on the grain.

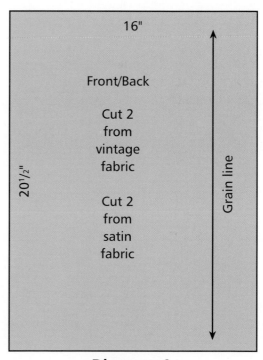

16"

Front/Back

Cut 2 from vintage fabric

Cut 2 from satin fabric

20$^1/_2$"

Grain line

Diagram A

Cutting the Fabrics

1. Using scissors, cut the pattern pieces from the vintage fabric, simultaneously cutting two Sides, two Handles, one Front, and one Back.

2. Repeat Laying Out the Patterns: Steps 1–3 on page 49 and Step 1 above with satin fabric for the Lining.

3. Mark the Handle placements on the vintage Front and Back, using a fabric-marking pen or pencil, as shown in Diagram B below.

Mark the Button placements on the satin Back as shown in Diagram B.

Mark the Buttonhole placements on the vintage Front as shown in Diagram B.

Mark the vintage and satin Sides at bottom dot as shown on the Sides Pattern on page 54.

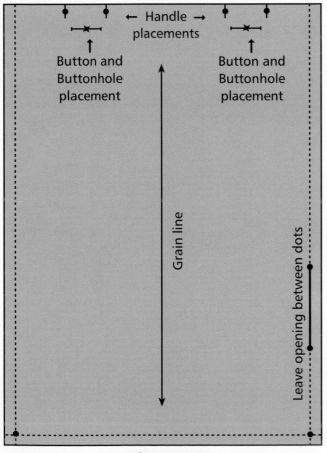

Diagram B

Mark a 4" opening on one satin Back and on one Side where the fabric will be left open for turning as shown in Diagram B at left and on the Sides Pattern.

Sewing the Seams

1. Using the vintage fabric pieces, place the Front and Back, right sides together, aligning the bottom edges.

2. Refer to Technique 3: Sewing the Long Edges, Step 2 on page 33.

3. Refer to the Glossary: Backstitch on page 108. Backstitch to lock the stitches.

Refer to the Glossary: Stitch on page 108. Stitch the seam line, using a $1/2$" seam allowance. Remove the pins as you stitch.

4. Press the seam allowance open.

5. Place one Side over one edge of the Front and Back, right sides together, aligning the bottom center mark on the Side to the seam line on the Front and Back at the dots. Pin together.

6. Stitch the seam line, using a $1/2$" seam allowance. Repeat with the remaining side. Press the seam allowances open.

7. Turn the handbag right side out.

8. To sew the lining, repeat Steps 1–6 above, using the satin fabric pieces and making certain to leave an opening on one of the seams as shown on the Sides Pattern. Do not turn the lining right side out.

9. For one of the Handles, place the vintage fabric Handle over the satin fabric Handle, right sides together, aligning both long edges.

Pin the two pieces together.

10. Stitch the long edges, using a $1/2$" seam allowance.

11. Trim the seam allowances to $1/4$".

12. Refer to Technique 2: Finishing the Pillow, Step 2 on page 30. Edge-press the seam allowances open.

13. Using a large safety pin, turn the Handle right side out by attaching the safety pin to one short edge to use as the lead. Push it through the Handle and maneuver the fabric within itself until the Handle has been turned right side out.

14. With the seams at the sides, press the edges of the Handle.

15. Refer to the Glossary: Topstitch on page 108. Topstitch ¼" from the long edges of the Handle.

16. Repeat Steps 9–15 on page 50 and above for the remaining Handle.

17. Refer to the Glossary: Machine baste stitch on page 108. Pin and baste-stitch the ends of one Handle in place on the Front and one Handle in place on the Back, aligning ends with the top edge of the handbag.

18. Slip the lining over the handbag, right sides together, aligning the top edges. Make certain the Handles are hidden within the fabric layers.

Pin and stitch around the top edge, aligning the seam lines, using a ½" seam allowance.

19. Edge-press the seam allowances open, then turn the handbag right side out through the opening in the lining Side.

20. Push the lining inside the handbag. Press the seam along the top edge of the handbag.

21. Refer to the Glossary: Slip stitch on page 107. Slip-stitch the opening in the lining closed. To do this, slip the needle into the vintage fabric at one end of opening at its folded edge, hiding the knot within the fold. Pick up a small amount of satin fabric directly opposite the needle exit point and along the seam line. Slip the needle back into the folded edge and pull the thread through. Continue in this manner, making stitches ¼" apart.

<table>
<tr><td>7
technique</td></tr>
</table>

How do I make machine-stitched buttonholes and sew on a button?

Most sewing machines have a prescribed method for stitching buttonholes to the best advantage. Thoroughly read your sewing machine's manual, as your sewing machine may have an automatic buttonholer.

Making the Buttonholes

1. In most cases, one half of the buttonhole is stitched forward, then bar-tacked, and the other half stitched backward, then bar-tacked. The inside length of the buttonhole is calculated at $1/8"$ longer than the diameter of the button as shown below.

Caution: Before sewing buttonholes on the finished project, practice on scrap fabric until you are comfortable and pleased with the results.

2. Make two buttonholes on the handbag Front.

Note: To accommodate the bulk of the fabric layers, use a wider stitch width.

3. Stitch over the buttonholes a second time as shown at top right.

Note: This will make very strong, well-defined buttonholes.

4. Using a seam ripper, make a "slit" between the parallel rows of stitching, from one end to the other as shown below.

Caution: Take precautions to avoid cutting through the bar tacks. Specialty buttonhole scissors can be purchased for this purpose.

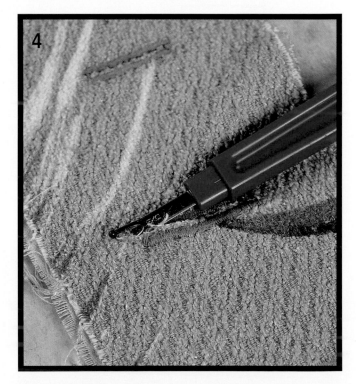

Adding the Buttons

1. Cut a 72"-length of thread. Double the thread and thread it through the eye of the hand-sewing needle as shown in Diagram C below. Knot all the thread ends together.

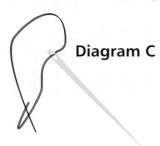

Diagram C

2. Slip the needle into the satin Back at the mark for the button placement. Take two small stitches at the mark.

3. Thread the needle through one of a button's holes, then down through the second hole as shown in Diagram D below.

Diagram D

4. Stitch through all fabric layers, then back up through the button. Pull the thread taut.

5. Repeat Steps 3 and 4 above several times, ending with the thread underneath the button.

6. Wrap the thread three times around the button stitches as shown in Diagram E below.

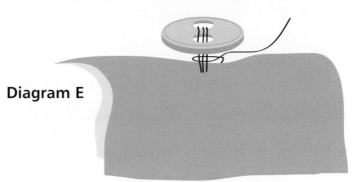

Diagram E

7. Wrap the thread around the button stitches once more, forming a loop as shown in Diagram F below. Slip the needle through the loop one time, then pull taut. Repeat this process two more times.

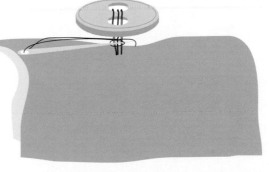

Diagram F

8. Take a small stitch next to the thread wraps, leaving a loop as shown in Diagram G below. Slip the needle through the loop two times and pull the thread taut. Take the needle back into the fabric next to the knot and out again 1" away. Cut the thread at the exit point to lose the thread end between the layers.

Diagram G

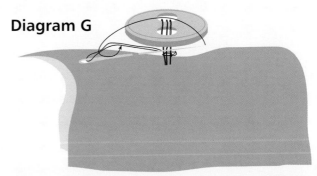

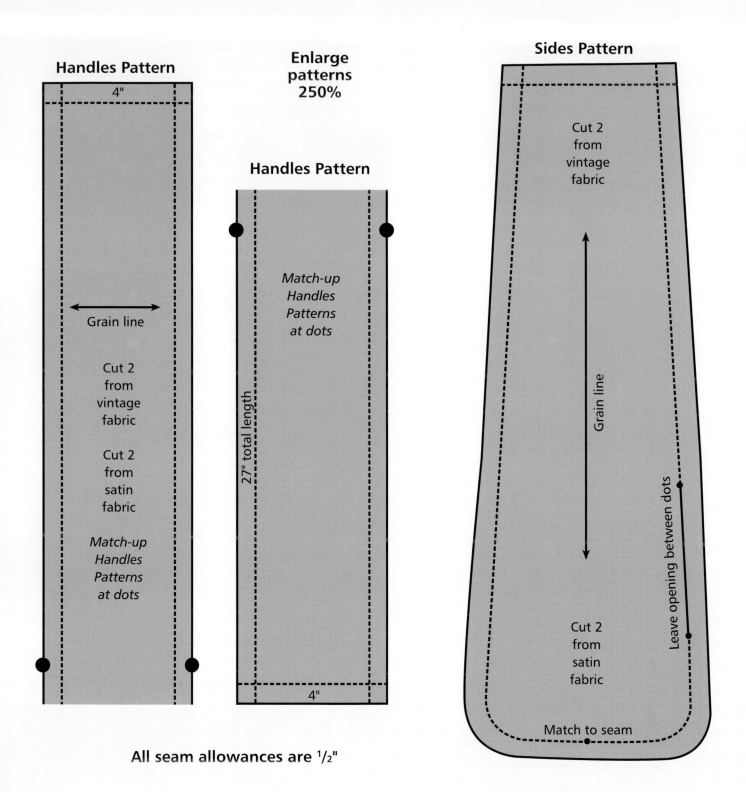

Handles Pattern

4"

Grain line

Cut 2
from
vintage
fabric

Cut 2
from
satin
fabric

*Match-up
Handles
Patterns
at dots*

**Enlarge
patterns
250%**

Handles Pattern

*Match-up
Handles
Patterns
at dots*

27" total length

4"

Sides Pattern

Cut 2
from
vintage
fabric

Grain line

Leave opening between dots

Cut 2
from
satin
fabric

Match to seam

All seam allowances are 1/2"

How do I form a gusset in a pillow and use stay-stitching to reinforce the seam line?

8 technique

8-9 techniques

Stay-stitching is a preliminary straight stitch placed at or close to the seam line prior to stitching a seam. It reinforces the seam line and helps maintain the shape and size of a seam, neckline, or other construction detail.

What You Will Need:

To make one pillow:

- Basic tools and supplies, see pages 12–21
- Brocade fabric, oriental pattern, 54"-wide (1/3 yard) for Front and Back
- Dupioni fabric, 44"-wide (1/8 yard) for Side Gussets
- Buttons, (3) 1 1/8"
- Polyester stuffing

Button-tufted Pillow

Here's How:

Cutting the Fabrics

1. Refer to How do I use a rotary cutter? on pages 22–23. Cut the brocade fabric for the Front and the Back of the pillow 9 1/2" wide x 14 1/2" long as shown in Diagram A at right.

Cut the dupioni fabric for the Side Gusset pieces 2" wide x 23" long as shown in Diagram B below.

Design Tip:
• *The tufting process is used for sewing eyes on soft sculpture and teddy bears.*

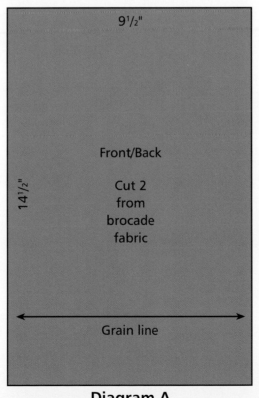

9 1/2"

14 1/2"

Front/Back

Cut 2 from brocade fabric

Grain line

Diagram A

Grain line

Side Gusset

23"

Cut 2 from dupioni fabric

2"

Diagram B

b
55

2. Mark the dots and squares on the Side Gusset pieces as shown in Diagram C at left.

Mark the button placement on the right side of the Front and the Back, using a fabric-marking pen or pencil as shown in Diagram D below.

Sewing the Seams

1. Pin the short edges of the Side Gusset pieces with straight pins placed vertically, right sides together, aligning the short edges.

2. Refer to the Glossary: Backstitch on page 108. Backstitch to lock the stitches.

Refer to the Glossary: Stitch on page 108. Stitch the short edges together, using a ¹/₂" seam allowance and stitching only between the dots. Remove the pins as you stitch.

3. Press the seam allowance open.

4. Refer to the Glossary: Stay stitch on page 108. Stay-stitch both long edges of the Side Gusset for a space of 1" on either side of the squares along the seam line.

5. Clip the seam allowance on both Side Gusset edges to the stay-stitching at the squares.

Note: By stitching only between the dots when joining the Side Gusset pieces and by clipping to the stay-stitching at the squares, the Side Gusset has been prepared to be sewn to the pillow Front and Back edges and corners.

6. Pin the Side Gusset to the Front, right sides together, matching a seam line and a square to each corner dot.

7. Stitch the seam line, using a ¹/₂" seam allowance, pivoting the fabric at each corner dot. Press the seam allowances toward the Side Gusset.

Diagram C

Side Gusset

Stay Stitch

Grain line

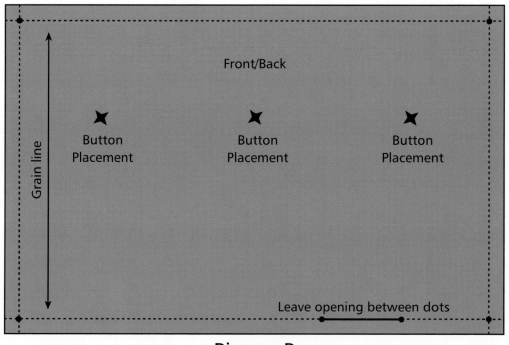

Front/Back

Button Placement   Button Placement   Button Placement

Grain line

Leave opening between dots

Diagram D

8. Using a point turner, accentuate each corner.

9. From the right side, fold and press the Front to the Side Gusset at the seam line. Refer to the Glossary: Edge stitch on page 108. Edge-stitch around the Front and Side Gusset of the pillow next to the seam line through all layers.

10. Repeat Step 5 on page 57 with the Side Gusset and the Back.

11. Repeat Step 6 on page 57, sewing the Side Gusset to the Back. However, in this seam line, an opening must be left for turning the pillow right side out. To do this, discontinue the stitching for a 4" space along one longer edge of the Back.

Finishing the Pillow

1. Refer to Technique 2: Finishing the Pillow, Step 4 on page 30. Turn the pillow cover right side out through the opening along the bottom.

2. Using a point turner, accentuate each corner.

3. From the right side, fold and press the Back to the Side Gusset at the seam line. Edge-stitch around the Back and Side Gusset of the pillow next to the seam line, except at the opening. Do not clip the threads.

4. Thread the thread ends into a hand-sewing needle, then stitch the threads in and out of the seam line. Refer to the Glossary: Lose thread ends on page 108. Lose the thread ends.

5. Firmly stuff the pillow with polyester stuffing through the opening.

6. Refer to the Glossary: Slip stitch on page 107. Slip-stitch the opening closed. To do this, slip the needle into the brocade fabric at one end of opening at the seam line, hiding the knot on the inside. Pick up a small amount of dupioni fabric directly opposite the needle exit point and along the seam line. Slip the needle back into the folded edge and pull the thread through. Continue in this manner, making stitches $1/4$" apart.

7. Edge-stitch over the slip-stitched area. Lose the thread ends.

How do I use buttons to tuft a pillow?

Tufting is a process done by sewing threads through a padded or stuffed surface. It was originally intended to hold padding in place, but now is commonly used as a decorative technique.

Button-tufting the Pillow

1. Cut a 72"-length of thread. Double the thread and thread it through the eye of the hand-sewing needle. Knot the thread ends together.

2. From the pillow Front, stitch through the pillow at the center mark, exiting at the center mark at the pillow Back. Stitch through the pillow again, directly next to the first stitch, this time from the Back to the Front.

3. Refer to Technique 7: Adding the Buttons on page 53. Slip the needle through the button, then securely stitch the button to the Front.

4. When the button is securely stitched to the Front, repeat Step 2 above. You will need to maneuver the needle around the button. Pull the thread taut. The pillow will begin to indent where sewn. Repeat one more time, pulling the thread taut, securing the "tufting."

5. Take the thread to the Back at the mark and knot the thread. Refer to the Glossary: Lose thread ends on page 108. Lose the thread ends.

6. Repeat Steps 1–5 above for the remaining two buttons.

How do I make a drawstring casing?

A drawstring casing is a created space in a garment, pillow, purse, or other accessory used to close an opening. When the casing is made so that a cord or ribbon is pulled from each side, the drawstring closes the opening simply and efficiently.

Pajama Bag

Here's How:

Cutting the Fabrics

1. Refer to How do I use a rotary cutter? on pages 22–23. Cut the fabric for the Bottom Section Front/Back (hereafter referred to as "A") 4" wide x 13" long as shown in Diagram A below.

Cut the fabric for the Middle Section Front/Back (hereafter referred to as "B") 5" wide x 13" long as shown in Diagram B below.

Cut the fabric for the Top Section/Lining Front/Back (hereafter referred to as "C") 23" wide x 13" long as shown in Diagram C on page 60.

What You Will Need:

To make one large pajama bag:

- Basic tools and supplies, see pages 12–21
- Cotton fabric, 44"-wide (1/8 yard) for Bottom Section
- Cotton fabric, 44" wide (1/4 yard) for Middle Section
- Cotton fabric, 44" wide (3/8 yard) for Top Section and Lining
- Ribbon, 1/2"-wide (1 1/2 yards)
- Child's socks, 1 pair
- Polyester stuffing

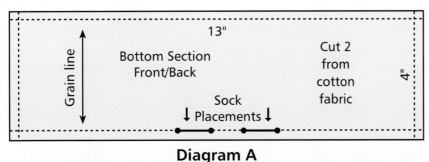

13"

Grain line

Bottom Section Front/Back

Cut 2 from cotton fabric

4"

Sock
↓ Placements ↓

Diagram A

13"

Grain line

Middle Section Front/Back

Cut 2 from cotton fabric

5"

Diagram B *Purple*

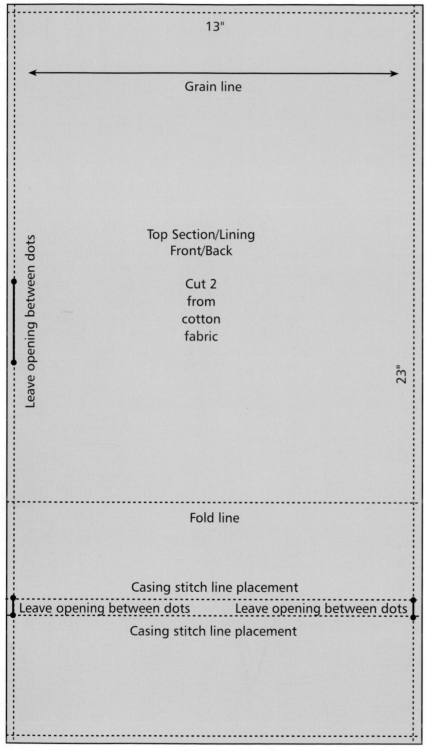

13"

Grain line

Top Section/Lining
Front/Back

Cut 2
from
cotton
fabric

Leave opening between dots

23"

Fold line

Casing stitch line placement

Leave opening between dots   Leave opening between dots

Casing stitch line placement

Diagram C

2. Mark the Fold line and the Casing stitch line placements on "C," using a fabric-marking pen or pencil, as shown in Diagram C at left.

Sewing the Seams

1. Pin the long edges of "A" and "B" Fronts with straight pins placed vertically, right sides together, aligning the long edges.

2. Refer to the Glossary: Backstitch on page 108. Backstitch to lock the stitches.

Refer to the Glossary: Stitch on page 108. Stitch the long edges together, using a $1/4$" seam allowance. Remove the pins as you stitch.

3. Press the seam allowance open.

4. Repeat Steps 1–3 above to sew "A" and "B" Backs together.

5. Repeat Steps 1–3 above to sew the long edges of "B" and "C" Fronts and Backs together.

Note: This will form the Pajama Bag Front with a self-lining.

6. Refer to Technique 4: Matching the Crossing Seams, Step 2, on page 39. Pin the Front to the Back, right sides together, matching the seams at the sides.

7. Stitch the side seam lines, using a $3/8$" seam allowance. However, in these seam lines, openings must be left for turning the pajama bag right side out and for the drawstring. To do this, discontinue the stitching for a 4" space along one side seam and for $1/2$" space on both side seams as shown in Diagram C at left. Press the seam allowances open.

8. Stuff the socks with polyester stuffing.

9. Pin the socks together along the ankle edges. Pin the top sides of the socks at the ankle edges to the bottom edge of "A" on the right side of the Front as shown in Diagram A on page 59 and in Diagram D below.

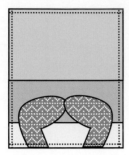

Diagram D

10. Refer to the Glossary: Machine baste stitch on page 108. Baste-stitch the socks in place, using a 1/4" seam allowance.

11. Pin the Front to the Back, right sides together, aligning the bottom edges.

12. Stitch the bottom seam line, using a 3/8" seam allowance, making certain to sew the socks into the seam. Press the seam allowance open.

Finishing the Pajama Bag

1. Refer to Technique 2: Finishing the Pillow, Step 1 on page 30. Clip the bulk from each corner.

2. Refer to Technique 2: Finishing the Pillow, Step 3 on page 30. Turn the pajama bag right side out through the opening along the side.

3. Using a point turner, accentuate each corner.

4. Refer to the Glossary: Slip stitch on page 107. Slip-stitch the opening closed. To do this, slip the needle into the Back fabric at one end of opening at the seam line, hiding the knot on the inside. Pick up a small amount of Front fabric directly opposite the needle exit point and along the seam line. Slip the needle back into the Back fabric at the seam line and pull the thread through. Continue in this manner, making stitches 1/4" apart.

5. Fold the lining portion of the fabric to the inside of the pajama bag along the Fold line as shown in Diagram C on page 60 and in Diagram E below and press.

6. Pin the lining in place.

7. Stitch both casing stitch lines from the outer side of the fabric, beginning at one of the side seams, and press.

8. Cut the ribbon into two equal lengths. Thread one length of ribbon through the eye of a ballpoint bodkin.

Beginning with the left side seam casing opening, slip the bodkin and the ribbon through the casing, exiting at the right side seam opening as shown in Diagram F below.

Repeat for the right side with the remaining length of ribbon.

Make certain both ribbon ends remain extended out of the opening and tie the ends of the ribbon at each side together.

9. Apply fray preventative to the ends of the ribbons.

Pull on both ribbons to close the top of the pajama bag.

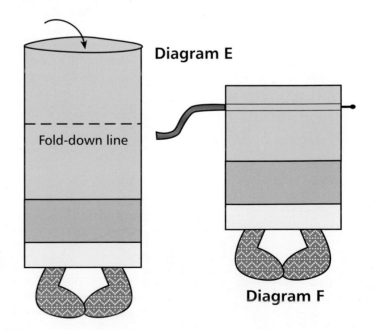

Diagram E

Fold-down line

Diagram F

How do I put in an exposed zipper?

Putting in an exposed zipper is an extremely simple introduction into the zipper world and is often used decoratively in handbags and sportswear. Other zipper applications include the centered, lapped, fly-front, invisible, separating, and dress side placket.

Zippered Pouch

Here's How:

Sewing the Seams and Adding the Zipper

1. Using scissors, cut the braid trims into 14$\frac{1}{2}$" lengths.

2. Beginning with the narrower of the two braid trims, fold in half and mark the center with a straight pin.

3. Place the zipper's top stop $\frac{1}{4}$" from the center mark so the edge of the braid trim lies against the coil edge as shown in Diagram A at right.

Pin the braid trim to the zipper tape with straight pins placed vertically.

4. Replace the standard sewing machine foot with the zipper foot and move the position of the needle to the far right.

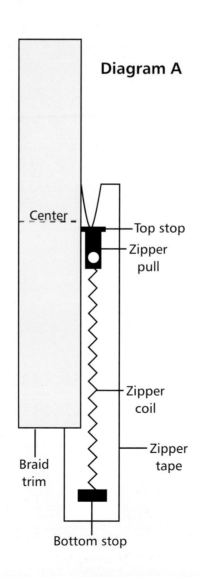

Diagram A

Center

Top stop

Zipper pull

Zipper coil

Zipper tape

Braid trim

Bottom stop

11
technique

What You Will Need:

To make one large zippered pouch:

- Basic tools and supplies, see pages 12–21
- Fancy braid trim, 2"-wide ($\frac{1}{2}$ yard) for Front and Back
- Fancy braid trim, 4$\frac{1}{2}$"-wide ($\frac{1}{2}$ yard) for Front and Back
- Cording, $\frac{1}{4}$"-wide (1 yard) for Handle
- Nylon zipper, 7"–9"
- Beaded fringe, 2"–4" long ($\frac{1}{8}$ yard)
- Silk ribbon, 4mm-wide ($\frac{1}{3}$ yard)

5. Refer to the Glossary: Backstitch on page 108. Backstitch to lock the stitches.

Refer to the Glossary: Stitch on page 108. Stitch the braid trim to the zipper tape, beginning at the center mark and placing the stitches as close to the braid trim's selvage edge as possible. Make certain to not stitch into the zipper's top stop. Remove the pins as you stitch.

6. Fold the remaining braid trim in half and mark the center with a straight pin.

7. Align the center and end of the wider braid trim with the center and end of the narrower braid trim, pinning it to the opposite edge of the zipper tape. Make certain the edge lies against the zipper coil.

8. With the position of the needle still to the far right, rotate the piece 180° in order to stitch the wider braid trim to the zipper tape as shown below.

9. Refer to the Glossary: Whipstitch on page 107. If the zipper needs to be shortened, beginning ³/₈" from the end of the braid trim, whipstitch tightly across the zipper coil 8–10 times, forming a new bottom stop as shown in Diagram B at right.

Trim away excess zipper, even with the braid trim.

10. At the upper end, tuck the zipper tabs to the inside at a 45° angle, hand-stitching the tabs in place so they are hidden from the outer side as shown in Diagram C below.

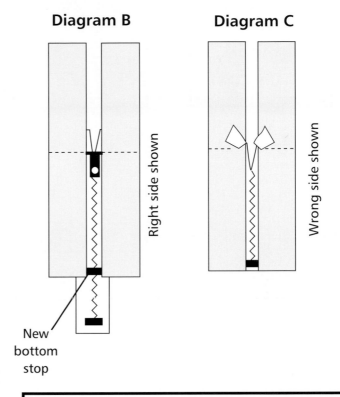

Diagram B **Diagram C**

Right side shown

Wrong side shown

New bottom stop

Tips:

• *Fabric-basting glue is great for placing the zipper in the seam before stitching. Test fabric for staining before applying glue.*

• *Lapped zippers are used for side seams and often for back seams of garments.*

• *Take care not to touch the zipper teeth of nylon zippers with a hot iron—they can melt.*

• *Some zippers are designed to not blend in with the project, but rather to become a design accent for it.*

11. Beginning at the center marks, whipstitch the remainder of the braid-trim's selvage edges together as shown at right and in Diagram D below.

12. Fold the braid trims in half, right sides together, matching the raw ends as shown in Diagram E below. Stitch, using a ¹/₂" seam allowance, easing the Front to fit the Back.

Press the seam allowances open.

Turn the pouch right side out and press flat with the seam allowances to one side.

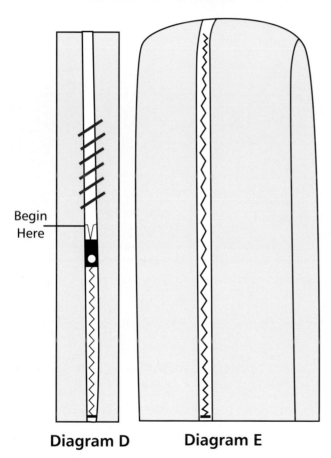

Begin Here

Diagram D   **Diagram E**

2. Refer to the Glossary: Zigzag stitch on page 108. Zigzag-stitch the top braid trim edges together, catching the handle ends. Zigzag-stitch the bottom braid trim edges together.

3. Tightly roll the length of the beaded fringe along the top zipper tape. Hand-stitch the "roll" to secure the shape.

4. Using silk ribbon, stitch the beaded fringe roll to the zipper pull.

Finishing the Pouch

1. Slip the cord handle ends within the top braid trim and pin to the upper edge, having ¹/₂" of braid trim within the pouch and placing the handle ends at the side folds as shown in Diagram F at right.

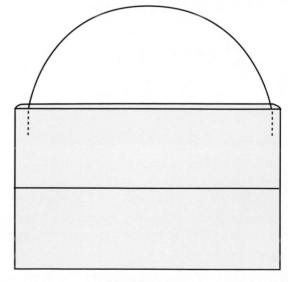

Diagram F

How do I finish an edge with bias binding?

Bias binding is a useful and decorative way to enclose raw edges. The binding can be purchased ready-made or made from your fabric of choice. For economical purposes, bias binding strips are pieced together.

Hanging Organizer

Here's How:

Preparing the Pattern

1. Enlarge the Front/Back Pattern on page 71 to 300%. Cut out the pattern.

Laying Out the Pattern

1. Refer to Technique 6: Laying Out the Patterns, Steps 2 and 3 on page 49. Pin the pattern to the quilted muslin fabric.

Cutting the Fabrics

1. Using scissors, cut the pattern piece from the quilted muslin fabric for the Front of the organizer.

2. Repeat Laying Out the Pattern, Step 1 and Cutting the Fabrics, Step 1 at left with the canvas fabric for the Back of the organizer.

3. Refer to How do I use a rotary cutter? on pages 22–23. Cut the chenille fabric for the Pocket 8" wide x 20" long as shown in Diagram A below.

4. Mark the Stitch line placements on the Front and the Pocket, using a fabric-marking pen or pencil, as shown in Diagram A.

Mark the dots on the Front at the seam allowance for the Ribbon placement as shown on the Front/Back Pattern.

What You Will Need:

To make one organizer:

- Basic tools and supplies, see pages 12–21
- Quilted muslin fabric, 54"-wide (1/2 yard) for Front
- Canvas fabric, 54"-wide (1/2 yard) for Back
- Chenille fabric, 60"-wide (1/4 yard) for Pocket
- Cotton fabric, striped pattern, 44"-wide (1/2 yard) for Bias binding
- Lace corner, 9" scrap
- Ribbon, 1/4"-wide (2 yards)
- Ribbon, 1/2"-wide (1 yard)
- Buttons with shanks, (3) 5/8"
- Plastic ring, 3/4"-diameter for Hanger

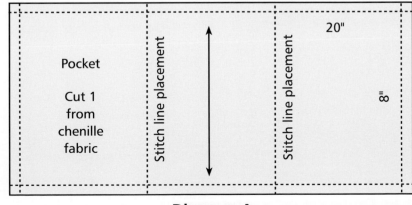

Diagram A

Cutting the Bias Binding

1. Refer to the Glossary: True bias on page 109. Find the true bias of the cotton fabric. To do this, fold a corner of the cotton fabric down so the selvage edge (lengthwise grain) meets the cut fabric edge at the crosswise grain, forming a 45° angle. Pin with straight pins to secure.

2. Using scissors, cut along the edge of the fold, then fold the bias cut over on itself.

3. Refer to How do I use a rotary cutter? on pages 22–23. Cut four 1½"-wide bias strips.

Note: As you are working with a piece of fabric that is 18"-wide, the bias-cut lengths should be about 24".

Embellishing the Front

1. Pin the lace corner to the top of the Front with straight pins placed vertically.

2. Refer to the Glossary: Topstitch on page 108. Topstitch the lacy edge of the lace corner. Remove the pins as you stitch.

3. Refer to the Glossary: Machine baste stitch on page 108. Baste-stitch the outer edges of the lace corner, using a ¼" seam allowance.

4. Pin the ¼"-wide ribbon onto the Front as shown on the Front/Back Pattern.

5. Baste-stitch in place.

Sewing the Seams

1. Place the Front over the Back, wrong sides together, aligning all edges.

2. Pin the two layers together.

3. Baste-stitch, using a ¼" seam allowance, and press.

Adding Bias Binding to the Pocket

1. Refer to the Glossary: Backstitch on page 108. Backstitch to lock the stitches.

Refer to the Glossary: Stitch on page 108. Working with one bias strip, pin and stitch the bias binding to the top edge of the Pocket, right sides together, using a ³/₈" seam allowance as shown below.

2. Press the seam allowance toward the bias binding.

3. With the pocket wrong side up, press the remaining edge of the bias binding down ½" to the wrong side. Fold the bias binding over the top edge of the pocket seam, encasing the seam, and pin in place as shown below.

Note: The turned-under edge should be placed just beyond the first seam.

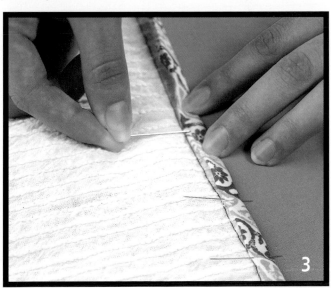

4. Refer to the Glossary: Edge stitch on page 108. Working from the right side, edge-stitch the bias binding through all thicknesses just to the inside of the seam.

Make certain to catch the turned-under edge on the wrong side of the Pocket and press.

5. Fold the Pocket on the solid lines to meet the dotted lines, forming an inverted box pleat.

Pin and baste-stitch the pleats in place along the bottom edge of the Pocket.

Sewing the Pocket to the Organizer

1. Pin the Pocket to the Front, aligning the bottom and both side edges, and matching the Stitch lines on the Front to the Stitch lines on the Pocket at the top and bottom edges.

2. Stitch the Pocket in place at the Stitch lines.

Making the Hanger

1. Working with a 3" scrap of bias binding, press under the bias edges ¹/₂", then press in half.

2. Slip the pressed bias binding through the plastic ring.

Pin the ends together.

3. Pin and baste-stitch the edges of the bias binding to the right side of the Back at the center top.

Adding Bias Binding Around the Organizer

1. Stitch together the remaining strips of bias binding. To do this, the short edges from two bias pieces must have a 45° angle along the grain line as shown in Diagram B below.

If necessary, trim the short bias edges to match the grain line, then place the edges, right sides together, and stitch, using a ¹/₄" seam allowance.

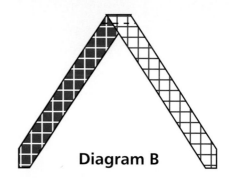

Diagram B

2. Press the seam allowances open.

3. Working from the Front, pin and stitch the bias binding to the sides and top of the organizer through all thicknesses, beginning with the bottom left corner, using a ³/₈" seam allowance.

4. Press the seam allowances toward the bias.

5. Working with the Back side up, press the remaining edge of the bias binding down ¹/₂" to the wrong side. Fold the bias binding over the edges of the organizer, encasing the seam, and pin in place.

6. Working from the right side, edge-stitch the bias binding through all thicknesses just to the inside of the seam.

Make certain to catch the turned-under edge on the back side of the organizer and press.

7. Repeat Steps 3 and 4 above, stitching the bias to the bottom edge of the organizer, leaving a ¹/₂" seam allowance of bias binding at the beginning and the ending of the bottom edge.

8. Repeat Steps 5 and 6 above.

9. Before pinning in place, fold in the bias binding side edges even with the finished side edge. Fold the bias binding again to encase the seam.

10. Pin and edge-stitch from the front side.

11. Refer to the Glossary: Slip stitch on page 107. Slip-stitch the fabric edges of the hanger to the Back at the center top.

Finishing the Organizer

1. Knot the ribbon at both ends. Slip the 1/2"-wide ribbon through the plastic ring and tie into a small bow.

2. Add the buttons as shown on the Front/Back Pattern.

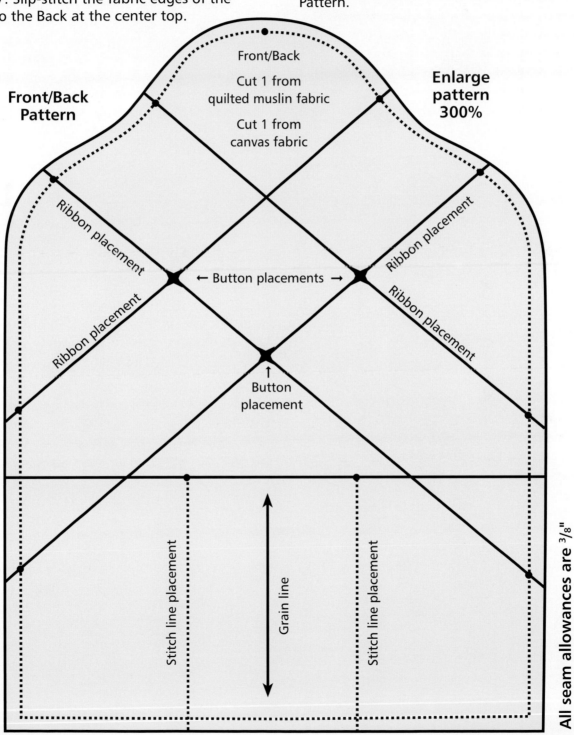

Front/Back

Cut 1 from quilted muslin fabric

Cut 1 from canvas fabric

Front/Back Pattern

Enlarge pattern 300%

Ribbon placement

Ribbon placement

Ribbon placement

Ribbon placement

← Button placements →

↑ Button placement

Stitch line placement

Stitch line placement

Grain line

All seam allowances are 3/8"

How do I make a ruffle?

Ruffles are in and out of fashion, both for clothing and home decorating. They are a good sewing basic to learn about. Most important to remember is to adjust the gathers evenly and to not allow portions of the ruffle to be accidentally caught up in its own seam.

What You Will Need:

To make one pillow with ruffles:

- Basic tools and supplies, see pages 12–21
- Dupioni fabric, 44"-wide ($3/8$ yard) for Front and Back
- Krinkle fabric, 44"-wide ($1/2$ yard) for Ruffles
- Fusible interfacing, lightweight ($1/4$ yard) for Front

Ruffled Pillow

Here's How:

Preparing the Pattern

1. Enlarge the Pillow Pattern on page 76 to 150%. Cut out the pattern.

Laying Out the Pattern

1. Refer to Technique 6: Laying Out the Patterns, Steps 1–3 on page 49. Pin the pattern to the dupioni fabric.

Cutting the Fabrics

1. Using scissors, cut the pattern piece from the dupioni fabric, simultaneously cutting one Front and one Back.

2. Refer to How do I use a rotary cutter? on pages 22–23. Cut four 2" wide x 44" long strips from the krinkle fabric for the Applied Ruffle.

3. Cut two $2^1/2$" wide x 44" long strips from the krinkle fabric for the Inserted Ruffle.

4. Mark the Back where the fabric is to be left open for turning, using a fabric-marking pen or pencil, as shown on the Pillow Pattern.

5. Fold the Front in half, then in quarters, and press.

Mark the outer edge of the Front at the quarter marks as shown on the Pillow Pattern.

6. Beginning with the smallest, trace the four circles onto the Front for the Applied Ruffles placement, as shown on the Pillow Pattern, using a permanent ink pen.

7. Heat-set the ink by pressing over the ink with a hot iron.

8. Position the Pillow Pattern on the fusible interfacing and cut out one circle.

Trim the diameter of the circle by $1/2$".

Hemming and Gathering the Ruffle Strips

1. Fuse the interfacing to the wrong side of the Front.

2. Using the roll-hemmer foot and working with one Applied Ruffle strip at a time, wrong side up, roll-hem one long edge, beginning and ending at the selvage ends. To do this, lower the roll-hemmer foot and sew three stitches.

Use the beginning threads to pull the fabric into the scroll of the hemmer. The threads will be at the front of the foot. Place the threads on the right side.

Begin sewing the rolled hem while simultaneously folding the fabric up approximately 1/4" as it feeds into the hemmer scroll.

3. Narrowly hem the selvage ends.

4. Press the hem.

5. Repeat Steps 1–4 above with the remaining Applied Ruffle strips.

6. Remove the roll-hemmer foot and replace it with the standard foot.

7. Change the stitch length to 4.5, which is the length needed for hand-pulled gathering.

8. Working with the strip wrong side up, fold the remaining long edge over 1/4" and stitch close to the fold with the long stitches.

Stitch again 1/16" to the left of the first row. When two rows of gather stitches are pulled, the gathered fabric has a directed appearance and is much easier to control.

9. Repeat with the remaining Applied Ruffle strips.

Note: Working with the individual lengths and applying them one at a time is much easier than seaming the four lengths together and working them as one.

Applying the Ruffle

1. From each end, pull the threads to gather one fabric strip until the gathered edge measures 20".

Knot the threads at each end.

2. Trim and then thread the ends into a hand-sewing needle. Refer to the Glossary: Lose thread ends on page 108. Lose the threads within the gathers and trim off.

3. Beginning with the 7" outer circle, pin the gathered edge of one strip to the circle. Add another gathered strip, overlapping 1/2" onto the first strip. When the outer circle is complete, begin tapering the gathered strip so it starts to encircle the 5" circle. Continue adding and tapering the gathered strips onto the 5" and 3" circles.

Refer to the Glossary: Zigzag stitch on page 108. Zigzag-stitch in place as each row is encircled, using a narrow-sized stitch. Taper the end of the last gathered strip to the center of the pillow as shown below.

4. Refer to the Glossary: Hand stitch on page 107. Coil the remaining Applied Ruffle and hand-stitch it to the center of the pillow, forming a "rose."

Inserting the Ruffle

1. Stitch the Inserted Ruffle strips together at the short edges, using a 1/4" seam allowance. Stitch the ends together, forming a large circle.

2. Press the seam allowances open.

3. Remove the standard foot and replace it with the roll-hemmer foot.

4. Beginning near the seam, but not at the seam, roll-hem one long edge of the circle.

When stitches are joined in a circular piece of fabric, remove the beginning stitches. This can be done once you have hemmed enough fabric that the stitches can be removed without taking the fabric out of the hemmer. When the stitches meet the starting point, you will be able to finish the hem without an interruption in stitch appearance.

5. Press the hem.

6. Repeat Steps 6 and 7 at left.

7. Working with the circle wrong side up and beginning at a seam, stitch the gather stitches, using a $1/2$" seam allowance.

Stitch again $1/8$" to the right of the first row.

8. Mark the gather-stitched edge at quarter intervals by folding the Inserted Ruffle in half, then in half again. Place a straight pin in the seams at the folds.

9. In order to stitch the Inserted Ruffle to the outer pillow edge, the outer Applied Ruffle must be tucked under and pinned out of the way.

Note: If it is not pinned out of the way it could be caught up in the outer Inserted Ruffle seam.

10. Match and pin the circle to the pillow Front at the quarter marks, right sides together, with straight pins placed vertically.

Position the circle so the gather-stitched raw edge is aligned with the outer edge of the Front.

11. Gently pull the threads in both directions to gather the circle so it fits the outer edge of the Front. When the circle fits the edge of the Front, wrap the gathering threads around the straight pins to keep the gathers from coming undone.

12. Evenly adjust the ruffle gathers.

13. Refer to the Glossary: Backstitch on page 108. Backstitch to lock the stitches.

Refer to the Glossary: Stitch on page 108. Stitch the ruffle to the Front, placing the stitches just to the left of the outermost gathered edge. Remove the pins as you stitch.

Note: This is done so the gathering stitches will not show outside of the seam.

Finishing the Pillow

1. Refer to the Glossary: Stay stitch on page 108. Stay-stitch the Back between the squares along the seam line.

2. Refer to the Glossary: Clipping on page 106. Clip the seam allowance on the Back edges to the stay-stitching at the dots.

3. Pin the ruffle down over the Front so that parts of the ruffle will not be caught up in the outer edge seam.

4. Pin the Front to the Back, right sides together. The ruffled layers will be a little bulky.

5. Working from the Front, stitch the Front to the Back directly over the stitches from Step 13 at left. However, in this seam line, an opening must be left for turning the pillow right side out. To do this, discontinue the stitching between the dots where the Back was stay-stitched.

Stitch again $1/4$" to the right of the first row of stitches.

6. Trim the seam allowance just to the right of the second row of stitches. Before turning right side out, press the stay-stitched edge under.

7. Refer to Technique 2: Finishing the Pillow, Step 4 on page 30. Turn the pillow right side out through the opening along the seam.

8. Fluff all of the ruffles.

9. Firmly stuff the pillow with polyester stuffing through the opening.

10. Refer to the Glossary: Slip stitch on page 107. Slip-stitch the opening closed. To do this, slip the needle into the Back fabric at one end of opening at its folded edge, hiding the knot within the fold. Pick up a small amount of Front fabric directly opposite the needle exit point and along the seam line. Slip the needle back into the folded edge and pull the thread through. Continue in this manner, making stitches $1/4$" apart.

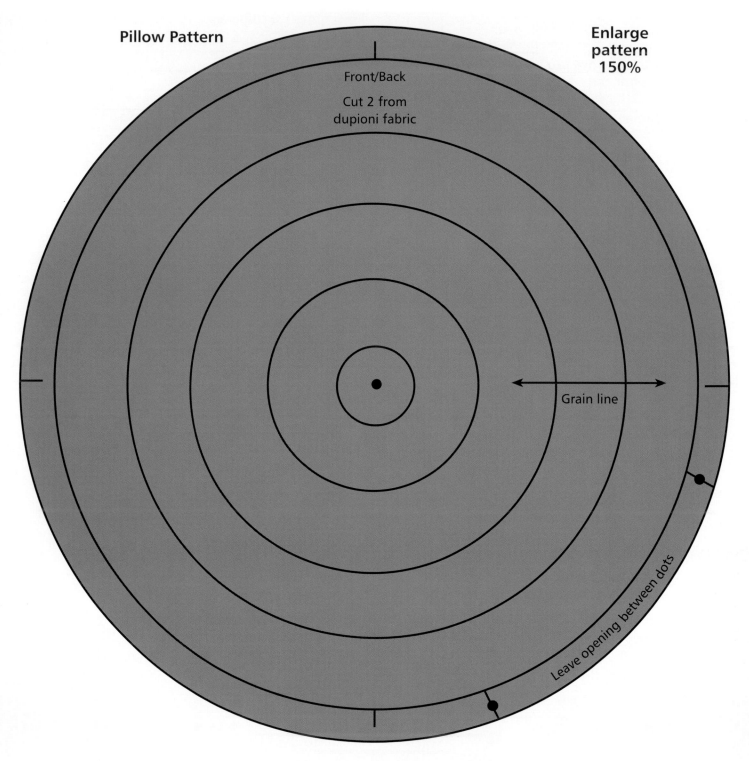

Pillow Pattern

Enlarge pattern 150%

Front/Back

Cut 2 from dupioni fabric

Grain line

Leave opening between dots

All seam allowances are ¹/₂"

How do I use a commercial pattern by following the pattern guide?

Pattern companies have been producing detailed patterns for over 100 years. The pattern envelope and inner guide give detailed information on fabric and notions needed, cutting layout, general sewing infor-mation, and detailed sewing instructions for the specific design purchased.

Child's Sundress

Here's How:

Preparing the Patterns

1. Read the pattern envelope and purchase the fabric and notions required.

2. Read through the entire pattern guide, including the basic reference information, cutting layouts, and sewing directions.

Laying Out the Patterns

1. Collect all the necessary pattern pieces and place them with the fabrics from which they are to be cut.

2. Refer to Technique 6: Laying Out the Patterns, Step 3 on page 49. Pin the pattern pieces in place.

Note: If the fabric and pattern lengthwise grain lines are not properly aligned, the garment will hang askew.

3. Pin the remainder of the pattern pieces to the appropriate fabrics by smoothing the pattern pieces from the center along the fabric to the outer edges as shown at left.

What You Will Need:

To make one child-sized sundress:

- Basic tools and supplies, see pages 12–21
- Commercial pattern, child's sundress
- Chenille fabric, medium green, 60"-wide ($^3/_8$ yard) for Bodice Front/Back
- Cotton fabric, gingham check, 44"-wide ($^3/_8$ yard) for Bodice Front/Back Lining
- Handkerchief, floral pattern, 12"-square for Bodice Front Trim
- Embroidered fabric, floral pattern, scraps, for Shoulder Straps
- Vintage fabric (tablecloth), floral pattern, 40"-square for Skirt Front/Back and Skirt Back Facing
- Eyelet trim, light green, 3"-wide (2 yards) for Skirt Trim
- Fusible interfacing, lightweight ($^1/_8$ yard) for Bodice Backs at the buttonholes and Skirt Back Facing
- Buttons, (3) $^1/_2$"; (2) $^3/_4$"
- Hook and eye

Cutting the Fabrics

1. Using scissors, cut out the pattern pieces from the fabrics, simultaneously cutting a left side and a right side of each pattern piece including those pieces placed on the fold.

Note: To help determine where the seams match up to each other, make certain to cut each outward notch. Transfer all pattern construction marks to the fabrics, placing all markings on the wrong side of the fabrics, except buttonholes and button placement.

2. Mark the darts, shoulder strap placements, and center fronts along the top and bottom edges of the Bodice Front and Bodice Front Lining by placing a straight pin through the pattern and the fabric.

3. Lift the pattern away from the fabric, except at the pinned construction marks. Mark each construction mark on the wrong side of the fabric, using a fabric-marking pen or pencil as shown below.

Mark the buttonhole placement and center back along the top and bottom edges of the Bodice Back and Bodice Back Lining.

Note: Make certain to mark both fabric layers on the wrong sides of the fabrics. Do not remove the pattern piece entirely until you are stitching that piece.

4. Mark the button placement on the right side of the Shoulder Strap. Mark the Skirt Back Facing as indicated on the pattern.

5. Mark the center Front/Back along the top edge and the pleat fold line on the Skirt Front/Back.

Transfer all marks as indicated on the pattern, marking buttonhole placement on the Right Skirt Back.

Sewing the Bodice

1. Fold the Bodice Front, right sides together, along the center dart lines. Pin the darts horizontally, aligning dots. Mark the beginning and ending of the darts with straight pins. Using a ruler and a fabric-marking pen or pencil, connect the dots.

Refer to the Glossary: Backstitch on page 108. Backstitch to lock the stitches.

Refer to the Glossary: Stitch on page 108. Stitch along the lines. Begin stitching each dart at its widest point, backstitching at the beginning. Decrease the stitch size at the end of each dart, eliminating the need to backstitch. Remove the pins as you stitch.

Note: As you gain confidence in your sewing, your eye can "draw the line" between dots.

Press the darts toward the center. Darts are always stitched and pressed before proceeding with major construction seams.

2. Stitch the darts on the Bodice Front Lining.

3. Pin a corner of the handkerchief to the right side of the Bodice Front, aligning the corner point with the center.

Refer to the Glossary: Machine baste stitch on page 108. Baste-stitch the top edges together.

Refer to the Glossary: Topstitch on page 108. Topstitch the corner edges in place as shown below. Trim away excess handkerchief.

4. Stitch the Shoulder Straps, right sides together, using a $5/8"$ seam allowance.

5. Refer to Technique 2: Finishing the Pillow, Step 1 on page 30. Clip the bulk from each corner and trim the seams to $1/4"$.

6. Refer to Technique 2: Finishing the Pillow, Step 2 on page 30. Edge-press the seam allowances open.

7. Using a large safety pin, turn the Shoulder Straps right side out by attaching the safety pin to one short edge to use as the lead. Push it through the Shoulder Strap and maneuver the fabric within itself until the Shoulder Strap has been turned right side out.

8. Matching the marks, pin and baste-stitch in place on the Bodice Front.

9. Reinforce the buttonholes on the Left and Right Bodice Backs. To do this, fuse a 1" square of interfacing to the wrong side of the fabric over each buttonhole mark, following manufacturer's directions.

10. Stitch the Bodice Front to the Bodice Back at the sides. Repeat with the Bodice Front/Back Linings.

11. Press the seam allowances open.

12. Pin the Bodice Lining to the bodice, right sides together, aligning notches, centers, and seams.

13. Stitch the back, armhole, and front neck edges as shown below.

14. Trim the seams to $1/4"$. Clip the curves and trim the bulk from each corner as shown below.

15. Edge-press the seam allowances open.

16. Turn the bodice right side out and press.

17. Baste-stitch the lower edges together.

Sewing the Skirt

1. Reinforce the Skirt Back center back seam at the circle by stitching about 1" in both directions of the circle on the $5/8$" seam allowance line.

2. Stitch the Skirt Back center back seam to the circle.

Clip the seam diagonally to the circle, then trim the seam below the circle to $1/4$".

3. Refer to the Glossary: Zigzag stitch on page 108. Zigzag-stitch the seam. Press the seam to one side.

4. Fuse the Skirt Back Facing interfacing to the wrong side of the vintage Skirt Back Facing. Stitch the Skirt Back Facing center seam line from the lower edge to the circle.

Clip the seam diagonally to the circle.

Press the seam allowance open.

Zigzag-stitch the outer edge of the Skirt Back Facing.

Pin the Skirt Back Facing to the Skirt Back, right sides together, aligning raw edges, circles, and seams.

5. Stitch from the upper edges to the circle as shown below.

6. Trim the seams and clip the curves.

7. Edge-press the seam allowances open.

8. Turn Skirt Back Facing to the inside and press.

9. Lap the Right Skirt over the Left Skirt, aligning centers.

Topstitch on the outside from the circle to the square through the overlapped layers.

10. Refer to Technique 4: Finishing the Seams with a French Seam and Narrow Machine-hemming, Steps 2–4 on page 45. Stitch the Skirt Front to the Skirt Back, using French seams.

11. Press the seams toward the back.

12. Measure the skirt hem width. Cut the eyelet trim to this measurement plus 1".

Stitch the trim together at the ends, using a $1/2$" seam allowance.

Press the seam allowance open.

Stitch the trim to the bottom edge of the skirt, right sides together, using a $5/8$" seam allowance, aligning the trim seam with the center back seam.

Trim the seam to $1/4$" and zigzag-stitch the trimmed edge.

Press the seam toward the skirt.

13. To make pleats at the upper edge of the skirt, bring the dotted line to a solid line in the direction of the arrows. Pin and baste-stitch the pleats in place as shown below.

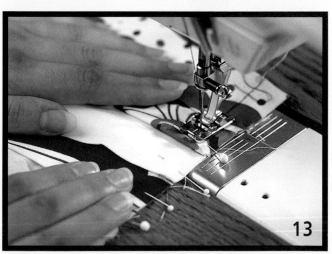

14. Pin and stitch the bodice to the skirt, right sides together, aligning the center fronts, seams, and back edge of the bodice at the skirt center back as shown below, having turned the Skirt Back Facing over the outside of the seam.

Clip the seam allowance next to the finished edge of the Skirt Back Facing.

Trim the Skirt Back Facing and bodice/skirt seam to ³/₈".

Zigzag-stitch the seam.

Turn the Skirt Back Facing to the inside. Press the bodice/skirt seam toward the bodice and the Skirt Back Facing seam toward the skirt.

15. Refer to Glossary: Edge stitch on page 108. From the right side, edge-stitch the bodice close to the seam.

Making the Buttonholes

1. Refer to Technique 7: Making the Buttonholes, Steps 1–4 on page 52. Make the buttonholes on the Bodice Back and Right Skirt Back.

Adding the Buttons

1. Refer to Technique 7: Adding the Buttons, Steps 1–8 on page 53. Sew the buttons in place on the Shoulder Straps and on the Right Skirt Back.

Adding the Closure

1. Sew the hook to the inside of the Left Skirt Back at the center and the eye to the outside of the Right Skirt Back as shown below.

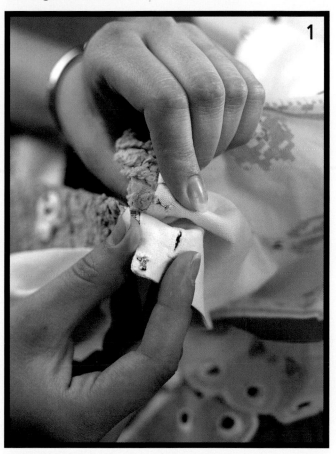

Design Tip: *Look for reproduction '40s-style printed tablecloth panels at your fabric store.*

15
technique

What You Will Need:

To make one heart:

- Basic tools and supplies, see pages 12–21
- Butcher paper
- Cross-dyed velvet fabric, 45"-wide (⅓ yard) for Front and Back
- Poly pellets
- Polyester stuffing
- Seed beads, 11/0
- Bias-cut ribbon, 1"-wide (½ yard)
- Decorative accessories

Design Tips:

- *Stencil velvet with metallic acrylic paint for an elegant treatment.*

How do I stitch velvet?

Velvet is a plush, luxurious fabric that has a surface depth called pile. Variations include velveteen, corduroy, velour, fleece, and fake fur. Fabrics with pile have a "nap," which means the fabric feels smoother in one direction than in the other. The nap affects the color and texture of the fabric—when the nap runs up (not smooth), the color is deeper and richer.

Velvet Heart

Here's How:

Creating the Pattern

1. Draw a heart, any shape and size, onto a piece of butcher paper. Cut out the pattern.

Laying Out the Pattern

1. Refer to Technique 6: Laying Out the Patterns, Steps 1–3 on page 49. Pin the pattern to the cross-dyed velvet fabric.

Note: Because the fabric is folded in half, the nap of the velvet will be running in the same direction. However, you may choose whether you want the nap to run up or down.

Cutting the Fabric

1. Using scissors, cut the pattern pieces from the velvet fabric, simultaneously cutting one Front and one Back.

2. Mark one side with a 3" space where the fabric is to be left open for turning, using a fabric-marking pen or pencil.

Sewing the Seams

1. Place the Front and Back, right sides together, aligning the bottom edges.

2. Refer to Technique 3: Sewing the Long Edges, Step 2 on page 33.

3. Refer to the Glossary: Hand baste stitch on page 107. Baste-stitch around the heart, using a 1/4" seam allowance. This will keep the velvet layers from sliding around. Remove the pins as you stitch.

4. Refer to the Glossary: Backstitch on page 108. Backstitch to lock the stitches.

Refer to the Glossary: Stitch on page 108. Stitch the seam line, using a 1/4" seam allowance, and making certain to leave an opening on one of the side seams.

5. Refer to Technique 2: Finishing the Pillow, Step 1 on page 30. Clip the bulk from the tip of the heart and around the curves. Clip the top center of the heart up to the seam line.

6. Refer to Technique 2: Finishing the Pillow, Step 2 on page 30. Edge-press the seam allowances open. Press the seam allowance under at the opening.

7. Refer to Technique 2: Finishing the Pillow, Step 4 on page 30. Turn the heart right side out through the opening along the side seam.

Finishing the Heart

1. Stuff the heart alternately with poly pellets and polyester stuffing through the opening until the heart is full, but soft.

2. Refer to the Glossary: Slip stitch on page 107. Slip-stitch the opening closed. To do this, slip the needle into the Back fabric at one end of opening at the seam line, hiding the knot on the inside. Pick up a small amount of Front fabric directly opposite the needle exit point and along the seam line. Slip the needle back into the Back edge and pull the thread through. Continue in this manner, making stitches 1/4" apart.

3. Cut a 72"-length of thread. Double the thread and thread it through the eye of the beading needle. Knot all the thread ends together.

Beginning where the heart was slip-stitched closed, slip the needle into the seam so the knot is hidden within the seam. Sew the seed beads around the heart at the seam line. To do this, take one tiny backstitch with the thread. Slip a seed bead onto the needle, take the backward stitch, then stitch forward again 1/4".

Repeat until beads surround the entire heart. Knot the thread at the end and trim off the excess.

4. Refer to the Glossary: Hand stitch on page 107. To embellish the heart, hand-stitch bias-cut ribbon and other decorative accessories as desired.

16
technique

What You Will Need:

To make one curtain:

Basic tools and supplies,
  see pages 12–21
Sheer fabric,
  36"- to 120"-wide
  (3 yards)
Masking tape

How do I stitch sheer fabric?

Sheer fabrics range in widths from 36"-wide for certain silk chiffon to 120"-wide for sheer drapery fabrics. Because it is lightweight, sheer fabric gathers down in width more than other fabrics. For window treatments, it is generally recommended to use at least two-to-one fullness for the window area to be covered.

Sheer Curtain

Here's How:

Measuring the Window and Cutting the Fabric

1. Measure the height of the window. Add 4" for the hem and $4\frac{1}{2}$" for the rod pocket and top ruffle.

Note: Add extra length if the curtain will be tied back and draped.

2. Refer to How do I use a rotary cutter? on pages 22–23. Cut the sheer fabric to the necessary dimensions and trim off the selvage edges.

Sewing the Seams

1. With the fabric wrong side up, press one long edge over $\frac{7}{8}$". Press the same edge over on itself a second time.

While pressing, pin in place with straight pins placed vertically.

2. Refer to the Glossary: Back-stitch on page 108. Backstitch to lock the stitches.

Refer to the Glossary: Stitch on page 108. With the fabric still wrong side up, stitch close to the inner folded edge to hem one side of the curtain and press. Remove the pins as you stitch.

3. Repeat Steps 1 and 2 above for the second long edge.

4. With the fabric wrong side up, press the bottom edge over 2". Press the same edge over on itself a second time.

While pressing, pin in place.

5. With the fabric still wrong side up, stitch close to the inner folded edge to hem the bottom of the curtain and press.

6. With the fabric wrong side up, press the top edge over $4\frac{1}{2}$".

Place a piece of masking tape 2" to the right of the sewing machine needle.

7. To make the top ruffle, align the top pressed edge of the curtain with the tape and stitch. The stitches should be 2" from the pressed edge.

8. Press the remaining edge under $1/2$". With the fabric still wrong side up, stitch close to the pressed-under edge, to form the rod pocket.

Hanging the Curtain

1. Mount the rod brackets to the sides of your window, following manufacturer's directions.

Slip the rod through the rod pocket and hang the rod on the brackets.

How do I stitch polar fleece fabric?

Fleece is widely available with different depths and textured piles. This fleece is known as sherpa, as it has a lamb-like quality to its pile.

This fabric does not require a seam finish; however, because the fabric is thick, the seams must be trimmed to $1/4$", then overcast or topstitched to eliminate the bulk.

What You Will Need:

To make one duck:

Basic tools and supplies, see pages 12–21

Sherpa fabric, 54"-wide ($1/4$ yard) for Duck Body

Wool felt scraps, aqua, light aqua, tan for Beak and Eyes

Sheer ribbon, $1 1/2$"-wide ($1 1/8$ yard) for Bow

Feathers for Tail and Top of Head

Embroidery flosses

Polyester stuffing

Fuzzy Ducky

Here's How:

Preparing the Pattern

1. Enlarge the Duck Pattern on page 92 to 150%. Cut out the pattern.

Laying Out the Pattern

1. Refer to Technique 6: Laying Out the Patterns, Steps 1–3 on page 49. Pin the pattern to the sherpa fabric.

Cutting the Fabric

1. Using scissors, cut the pattern piece from the sherpa fabric, simultaneously cutting one Body Front and one Body Back.

2. Cut two Beaks from the tan felt, two Eyes from the light aqua felt, and two Eyeballs from the aqua felt.

Sewing the Beak and Eyes in Place

1. Position one Beak on the Body Front as shown on the Duck Pattern and one Beak on the Body Back. Refer to the Glossary: Whipstitch on page 107. Whipstitch the Beaks in place along the inner edge, using two strands of embroidery floss.

On the inside, trim the Beaks $1/8$" from the stitching.

Whipstitch around the outside edges of the Beaks, using two strands of embroidery floss.

2. Place each Eyeball over each Eye, then position on the Body Front as shown on the Duck Pattern. Whipstitch in place, using two strands of embroidery floss.

Sewing the Seams

1. Pin the Body Front and the Body Back, wrong sides together, with straight pins placed vertically.

Slip a feather between the layers at the top of the head and pin in place. Slip another feather between the layers at the tail and pin in place.

2. Refer to the Glossary: Zigzag stitch on page 108. Zigzag-stitch the seam line, using a ⅛" seam allowance, making certain to leave an opening on one of the seams as shown on the Duck Pattern. Remove the pins as you stitch.

Finishing the Duck

1. Firmly stuff the duck with polyester stuffing through the opening.

2. Zigzag-stitch the opening closed.

3. Knot ribbon at each end. Tie the ribbon into a bow around the neck of the duck.

Tips:

• *On garments, a machine stretch stitch is recommended because it will stretch with the fabric rather than snap when stress is applied.*

• *Fleece has a nap. Make certain to lay pattern pieces so the nap runs one way, up or down for all pieces. If not laid this way, there will be a difference in the color of the pieces.*

**Duck
Pattern**

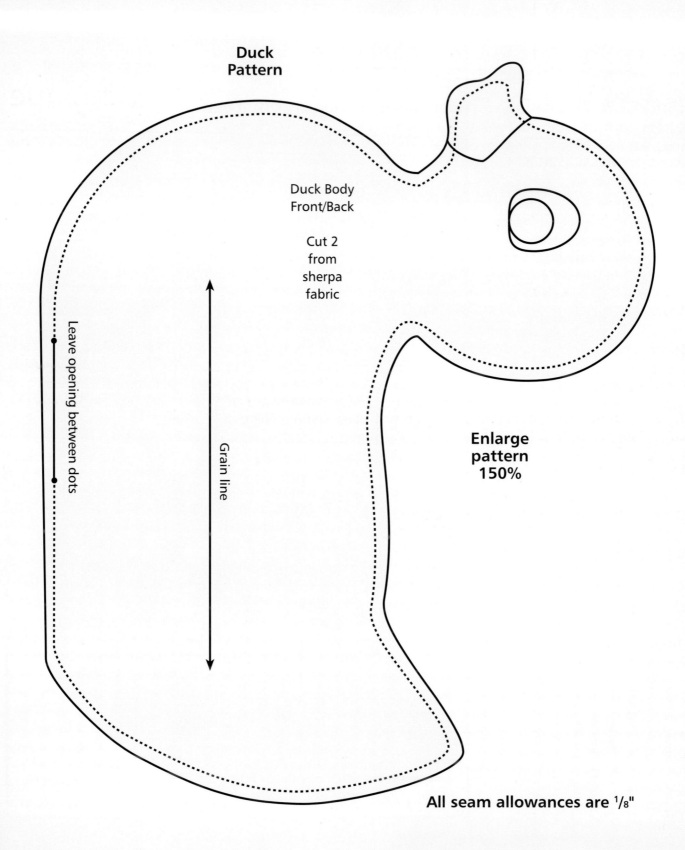

Duck Body
Front/Back

Cut 2
from
sherpa
fabric

Leave opening between dots

Grain line

**Enlarge
pattern
150%**

All seam allowances are 1/8"

How do I stitch fake fur fabric?

Fake furs are available with a variety of textures that can be as flat and plush as velvet or as wild as the "grouch." The eyelash fabric is a variation of the texture found on some fake furs. When working with eyelash fabric, make certain to move the eyelashes away from the seam when sewing.

What You Will Need:

To make one piano shawl:

- Basic tools and supplies, see pages 12–21
- Eyelash fabric, 44"-wide ($^3/_4$ yard) for Top
- Fake fur fabric, 54"-wide ($^1/_4$ yard) for Ends
- Dupioni fabric, 44"-wide ($1^3/_4$ yard) for Border

Piano Shawl

Here's How:

Cutting the Fabrics

1. Refer to How do I use a rotary cutter? on pages 22–23. Cut the eyelash fabric 25" wide x 44" long for the Top of the piano shawl.

Cut the fake fur fabric 25" wide x 9" long for the Ends.

Cut one 29" wide x 62" long strip from the dupioni fabric for the Back and two 25" wide x 2" strips from the dupioni fabric long for the Border.

Sewing the Ends and Border

1. Place the Top over the End, right sides together, aligning the 25" sides.

Note: Make certain to move the eyelashes away from the seam toward the left while sewing.

2. Pin the two layers together with straight pins placed vertically.

3. Refer to the Glossary: Backstitch on page 108. Backstitch to lock the stitches.

Refer to the Glossary: Stitch on page 108. Stitch the seam line, using a $^1/_2$" seam allowance as shown below. Remove the pins as you stitch.

4. Press the seam allowance toward the End.

5. Repeat Steps 1–4 on page 92 and above, sewing the remaining End to the Top.

Sewing the Long Edges

1. Refer to Technique 3: Sewing the Long Edges, Steps 1–5 on page 33. Stitch, using a $1/2$" seam allowance.

2. Press the seam toward the Back.

3. Repeat Steps 1–2 above, sewing the remaining long edge. However, in this seam line, an opening must be left for turning the piano shawl right side out. To do this, discontinue the stitching for a 5" space near the center.

4. Pin and stitch the 2"-wide Border strips to the Ends, aligning the 25" sides.

5. Press the seam allowances toward the Border.

6. Repeat Steps 1–5 above, sewing the remaining Border to the Ends.

Sewing the Short Edges

Note: Right sides should still be together.

1. Position the fabrics so the pieced Top is centered over the Back, with a 1" Border on both sides.

2. Pin and stitch one short edge, using a $1/2$" seam allowance.

3. Repeat Step 2 above, sewing the remaining short edge.

Finishing the Piano Shawl

1. Refer to Technique 2: Finishing the Pillow, Step 1 on page 30. Clip the bulk from each corner.

2. Refer to Technique 2: Finishing the Pillow, Step 2 on page 30. Edge-press the end seams.

3. Refer to Technique 2: Finishing the Pillow, Step 4 on page 30. Turn the piano shawl right side out through the opening along the side seam.

Note: If necessary, a straight pin can be used to gently capture and pull the fabric from the outside to help bring the corner out. Care must be taken not to pull the fabric threads.

4. Adjust the fabric so there is a 1" border along the side of the Back from the Front and press.

Because the seam allowance is pressed toward the Back, the Top at the seam line naturally slips underneath the 1" border at the seam line.

5. Thread the hand-sewing needle with a length of thread and knot the ends together.

6. Refer to the Glossary: Slip stitch on page 107. Slip-stitch the opening closed. To do this, slip the needle into the fabric at one end of opening at its folded edge, hiding the knot within the fold. Pick up a small amount of fabric directly opposite the needle exit point and along the seam line. Slip the needle back into the folded edge and pull the thread through. Continue in this manner, making stitches $1/4$" apart.

7. Refer to the Glossary: Topstitch on page 108. To help the piano shawl lie flat, topstitch around all edges close to the inner edge of the border.

Mary Jo Hiney

Section 3:
gallery

Mary Jo Hiney

Mary Jo Hiney works as a free-lance author and designer in the fabric and craft industry, gladly sharing skill-filled secrets gathered over a lifetime of experience.

Hiney loves to sew and loves to shop for fabric, especially in a classic-style fabric store filled with knowledgeable sales people.

She is an expert seamstress and credits her solid sewing foundation to her mom, who had learned to sew in junior high from a very strict teacher.

Hiney's designs focus on gifts and decorative accessories. Her one-of-a-kind pieces display beauty, enhanced with function.

Hiney is also the author of *The Beaded Object, Romantic Silk Ribbon Keepsakes, Two-Hour Vests, Beautiful Foundation-Pieced Quilt Blocks, Creating with Lace,* and *Fabulous Fabric Embellishments.*

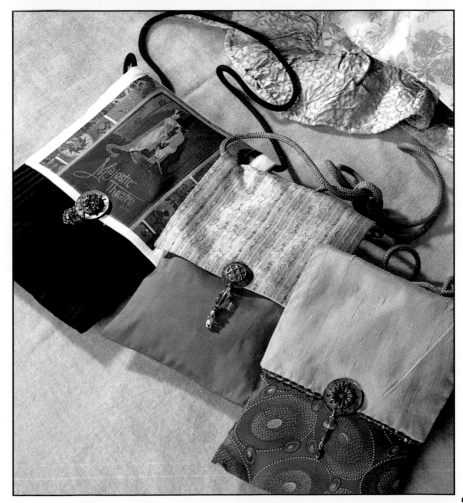

Tobi Klein Designs

Tobi Klein was born in New York in 1953. She received her MFA in painting with a concentration in Textile Design from Rochester Institute of Technology.

Leaving teaching after several years, and moving to Boston, led Klein to a position as manager of a gallery of American crafts. Soon after, Klein began designing jewelry and bags, using materials she had collected over the years, including buttons, trims, fabrics, etc.

Klein's work is continually evolving, most recently adding the silk and felt "keepers" to her line of evening bags. Her work is shown in galleries and is sold in shops throughout the United States.

Whimble Designs

Martha Young and her husband Jock McQuilkin are the cofounders of Whimble Designs, Inc.

Years ago, she began creating three-dimensional figures embellished with antique snippets of lace, buttons, and other interesting materials. She describes her artistic process as an "immersion in an elegant world of enchantment where one fantasy continually connects with the next," resulting in a glimpse of an ethereal and whimsical world.

Whimble Designs is a combination residence, studio, workshop, and retail gallery into which Martha's characters and stories are woven. Known also as "The Enchanted Place," it is Martha's vision made manifest where her beloved Whimbles work and play every day to help others realize their dreams. You can find patterns for these and more of Martha's whimsical creations in her book, *The World of Whimble Whimsey,* published by Sterling/Chapelle.

Anita Louise Crane

Anita Louise Crane has been designing, creating, photographing, painting, writing, and marketing since 1981.

Crane is best known for her original teddy bears. She has been a special-occasion and wedding dress designer and seamstress. In addition, she has been an artist-in-residence and proprietor of The Bearlace Cottage in Colorado Springs, Colorado, and then in Park City, Utah, which features her one-of-a-kind teddy bears as well as other collectibles, such as antique lace fashions, collectible antiques, laces, linens, and her paintings. She also is an accomplished watercolorist.

Crane lives in Park City, Utah, with her husband Bruce and kitty, Raisen. Her other interests are designing and creating decorative items for her home, such as lamp shades, slipcovers, window treatments, and decorative walls.

You can find patterns for these wonderful doll clothes in Crane's book *Two-Hour Dolls' Clothes* published by Sterling/Chapelle.

Glossary

Bar tack
Wider zigzag stitches at the top and bottom of a buttonhole.

Braid trim
A narrow, banded trim that can range in width from $1/8$" to 5" and beyond and includes embroidered, sequinned, or fringed bands and ribbon.

Breaking the stitch
Stopping the stitching process in a seam line. The process will include the $1/4$" backstitch, repositioning the needle, and beginning again with a $1/4$" backstitch at the new location.

Casing
A created space in a garment, pillow, purse, or other accessory used to close an opening.

Center back
A mark or line that indicates where a garment will fall at the center back of the body or at the center back of an accessory.

Center front
A mark or line that indicates where a garment will fall at the center front of the body or at the center front of an accessory.

Circle template
A plastic template with precut circles in sequential size ranges.

Clipping
A cut made in a seam allowance with scissors for various purposes. Do not cut through the seam allowance at any time.

Clipping bulk

Trimming fabric from the seam allowance of a corner by cutting diagonally across the corner, leaving $1/8$"–$1/4$" seam allowance. Trim some excess from the seam allowance near the corner as well.

Clipping curves

On an inward curve, make cuts into the seam allowance at $1/2$"–2" intervals. On an outward curve, cut small wedges into the seam allowance at $1/2$"–2" intervals. Allows a seam to lie flat when pressed, eliminating tension or pull.

Clipping to mark

Cutting into the seam allowance at a specific mark to aid in construction.

Clipping to seam

Cutting into the seam allowance to the seam line to aid in construction.

Crosswise grain

The direction of threads that run from selvage to selvage, at right angles to the lengthwise grain threads. Crosswise grain generally has a slight amount of give. Also known as Weft.

Dart

An angle of fabric stitched in a garment or accessory that provides fullness to a curved dimension such as the feminine form.

Easing

To reduce the slack in one layer to fit another.

Edge-pressing

A preliminary pressing step that exposes the seam line when turned right side out. It is used when it is not possible to press a seam allowance open.

Fold line

A marking that indicates where fabric is to be folded for construction purposes, such as for pleats and tucks.

Fuse

To adhere a product such as fusible interfacing to a fabric surface, using iron heat.

Grain

The lengthwise or crosswise direction of threads, which compose the fabric. See True bias, Crosswise grain, and Lengthwise grain.

Grain line

The direction of the lengthwise threads running parallel to the selvage. Place all grain line arrows along the lengthwise grain.

Gusset

A fabric piece inserted into a seam that provides ease, flair, or space.

Hand stitches:

• Hand baste stitch

See running stitch.

• Hand stitch

Stitching with small basic stitches as inconspicuously as possible.

• Running stitch

The most basic stitch, used for hand-gathering and hand-basting. With knotted thread and needle, weave the needle in and out of the fabric on the seam line, taking approximately $1/8$" long stitches. Pull on the thread to gather the fabric.

• Slip stitch

A hand-sewn stitch used for hems, sewing openings closed, attaching linings, and applying trims or fabrics. This stitch has an almost invisible application.

• Whipstitch

The thread is worked over a seam or edge diagonally with evenly spaced stitches. It was originally used to finish a seam prior to the invention of the zigzag stitch. Also known as an Overcast stitch.

Interfacings

A woven or nonwoven type of fabric that is primarily used to shape detail areas in a garment or an accessory. It adds body to the garment edges, cuffs, collars, and pockets, and prevents the stretching of necklines and buttonholes. Interfacings are categorized by their type of application, such as sew-in or fusible.

Lengthwise grain

The vertical, more sturdy threads which the crosswise threads are worked over and under. Also known as Warp.

Lining

A nearly duplicate copy of a garment or accessory that is sewn to the garment's inside and completely covers seam and construction details.

Lose thread ends

A method of hiding hand-sewn thread ends by stitching the needle into the fabric directly next to an ending knot, and then out again about 1" away. The thread is trimmed at the exit point and the thread end is hidden within the space.

Machine stitches:

• Backstitch

A preliminary step to stitching any seam, done by straight-stitching on the seam line forward $1/4$", then backward $1/4$", then forward to complete the seam. Begin and end every seam in this manner to lock the stitches. Backstitching is generally not used in piecing for quilt blocks.

• Edge stitch

A functional machine stitch that is placed very close to a finished edge worked from either the right or wrong side of the garment.

• Machine baste stitch

Preliminary stitching used to secure a construction piece in place before the seam has been stitched.

• Machine gather stitch

Double rows of stitches, using a larger stitch size. The first placed on the seam line; the second $1/16$"–$1/4$" in from the seam line. When a thread from each stitched row is gently pulled, the fabric gathers in soft folds.

• Stay stitch

Preliminary stitching used to maintain the original shape and size of a seam, neckline, or other construction detail.

• Stitch

The process of stitching any seam or detail with the natural forward movement of the sewing machine. Use the sewing machine's needle plate as a guide. Also known as a Straight stitch.

• Stitch in the ditch

A functional machine stitch that is placed on top of a seam that has been pressed to one side. The stitching controls a space without being visible.

• Straight stitch

See Stitch.

• Topstitch

A decorative machine stitch that is placed parallel to a seam or edge, worked from the right, or finished, side of the garment, with or without specialty thread.

• Zigzag stitch

The back and forth movement by a sewing machine used to overcast a seam allowance, preventing unraveling. It also can be used for decorative purposes.

Marking

The transfer of construction details from a pattern to the fabric, using any of several different fabric-marking pens, pencils, chalks, or transfer papers. Marking is done immediately after a project has been cut out.

Nap

The hairy, downy, or textured surface of a fabric such as velvet.

Narrow hem

A fine hem finish, $1/8$"–$1/4$" wide, suitable for sheers and when weight is not needed for a hem. It is achieved with a basic fold-over sewing technique or by using a roll-hemmer foot.

Notches

A wedge-shaped pattern marking along a seam line primarily found in commercial patterns, used for accuracy when aligning seams.

Overcast stitch

See Whipstitch.

Pattern cutting/sewing guide

A detailed guide found inside commercial pattern envelopes, along with full-sized patterns. The guide includes general sewing instructions, pattern marking interpretations, special instructions for the specific designs in the envelope, an encapsulated cutting guide for each design, and detailed sewing instructions for each design.

Place-on-fold bracket

A pattern marking that indicates that the center of the pattern is to be placed on the folded edge of the fabric. When cut, a left and right side of the pattern piece will automatically be cut from the fabric.

Pleat

A fold in the fabric made by doubling the fabric over on itself in various ways that provides controlled fullness or is used as a decorative application.

Poly pellets

A product used for stuffing dolls, toy parts, or pillows that adds weight and flexibility to the area being filled. Can be used along with polyester stuffing or alone.

Preshrunk

Fabric that has been washed and dried prior to its pattern pieces being cut out. This eliminates the concern that the finished item will shrink when washed. Before preshrinking, check the washing instructions, as some fabrics may only be dry-cleaned.

Press

Using an iron and ironing board to flatten seams and seam allowances and any construction aspect done concurrently with assembly and after assembly.

Press under

Pressing the designated amount along a raw edge over on itself, wrong sides together, creating a finished edge on the right side of the fabric.

Raw edge

The unfinished, cut edge of a piece of fabric.

Right sides together

Placing fabrics so the right, or finished, sides are facing each other.

Seam

A joining of two pieces of fabric with a line of stitches.

Seam allowance

The excess amount of fabric beyond the seam line, but not including the garment or accessory area.

Seam line

The exact line that a garment or accessory is to be stitched.

Self lining

A lining that is of or is an extension of the same material as the garment or accessory.

Selvage

The narrow, flat, woven border resulting along both lengthwise edges in the weaving process.

Stitch length

The size of a machine- or hand-sewn stitch.

Straight of grain

See Grain line.

Thread the needle

The process of inserting a thread end into the eye of a needle.

True bias

The diagonal intersection of the lengthwise and crosswise threads. Fabric cut on the bias grain possesses a great amount of give, similar to the stretch of a knit, but not with the elasticity of a knit. True bias exists at the 45° angle when lengthwise and crosswise grains are perpendicular.

Tuft

The process of sewing threads through a padded or stuffed surface, creating a permanent indentation.

Turn right side out

Turning a garment or accessory to the right, or finished, side.

Warp

See Lengthwise grain.

Weft

See Crosswise grain.

Wrong sides together

Placing fabrics so the wrong, or unfinished, sides are facing each other.

Acknowledgments

We would like to thank Prym-Dritz Corp. for providing the sewing notions used for the projects in this book.

Prym-Dritz Corporation
P.O. Box 5028
Spartanburg, SC 29304
(864) 576-5050
www.dritz.com

The Cotton Ball
475 Morro Bay Blvd.
Morro Bay, CA 93442
(800) 895-7402
www.thecottonball.com

Pfaff
610 Winters Ave.
Paramus, NJ 07653
www.pfaff-us-cda.com

Bernina
www.berninausa.com

We would also like to thank the artists who so graciously contributed projects to be featured in the gallery section of this book.

Bearlace Cottage
P.O. Box 702
Park City, UT 84060
(435) 649-8804
www.bearlace.com

Tobi Klein Designs
24 Windsor Street
Arlington, MA 02474
(617) 661-9595

Whimble Designs, Inc.
1540/42 Monroe Drive NE
Atlanta, Georgia 30324
(877) 944-6253
www.thewhimbles.com

Metric equivalency chart

INCHES TO MILLIMETRES AND CENTIMETRES

MM-Millimetres   CM-Centimetres

INCHES	MM	CM	INCHES	CM	INCHES	CM
$1/8$	3	0.9	9	22.9	30	76.2
$1/4$	6	0.6	10	25.4	31	78.7
$3/8$	10	1.0	11	27.9	32	81.3
$1/2$	13	1.3	12	30.5	33	83.8
$5/8$	16	1.6	13	33.0	34	86.4
$3/4$	19	1.9	14	35.6	35	88.9
$7/8$	22	2.2	15	38.1	36	91.4
1	25	2.5	16	40.6	37	94.0
$1^1/4$	32	3.2	17	43.2	38	96.5
$1^1/2$	38	3.8	18	45.7	39	99.1
$1^3/4$	44	4.4	19	48.3	40	101.6
2	51	5.1	20	50.8	41	104.1
$2^1/2$	64	6.4	21	53.3	42	106.7
3	76	7.6	22	55.9	43	109.2
$3^1/2$	89	8.9	23	58.4	44	111.8
4	102	10.2	24	61.0	45	114.3
$4^1/2$	114	11.4	25	63.5	46	116.8
5	127	12.7	26	66.0	47	119.4
6	152	15.2	27	68.6	48	121.9
7	178	17.8	28	71.1	49	124.5
8	203	20.3	29	73.7	50	127.0

YARDS TO METRES

YARDS	METRES	YARDS	METRES	YARDS	METRES	YARDS	METRES	YARDS	METRES
$1/8$	0.11	$2^1/8$	1.94	$4^1/8$	3.77	$6^1/8$	5.60	$8^1/8$	7.43
$1/4$	0.23	$2^1/4$	2.06	$4^1/4$	3.89	$6^1/4$	5.72	$8^1/4$	7.54
$3/8$	0.34	$2^3/8$	2.17	$4^3/8$	4.00	$6^3/8$	5.83	$8^3/8$	7.66
$1/2$	0.46	$2^1/2$	2.29	$4^1/2$	4.11	$6^1/2$	5.94	$8^1/2$	7.77
$5/8$	0.57	$2^5/8$	2.40	$4^5/8$	4.23	$6^5/8$	6.06	$8^5/8$	7.89
$3/4$	0.69	$2^3/4$	2.51	$4^3/4$	4.34	$6^3/4$	6.17	$8^3/4$	8.00
$7/8$	0.80	$2^7/8$	2.63	$4^7/8$	4.46	$6^7/8$	6.29	$8^7/8$	8.12
1	0.91	3	2.74	5	4.57	7	6.40	9	8.23
$1^1/8$	1.03	$3^1/8$	2.86	$5^1/8$	4.69	$7^1/8$	6.52	$9^1/8$	8.34
$1^1/4$	1.14	$3^1/4$	2.97	$5^1/4$	4.80	$7^1/4$	6.63	$9^1/4$	8.46
$1^3/8$	1.26	$3^3/8$	3.09	$5^3/8$	4.91	$7^3/8$	6.74	$9^3/8$	8.57
$1^1/2$	1.37	$3^1/2$	3.20	$5^1/2$	5.03	$7^1/2$	6.86	$9^1/2$	8.69
$1^5/8$	1.49	$3^5/8$	3.31	$5^5/8$	5.14	$7^5/8$	6.97	$9^5/8$	8.80
$1^3/4$	1.60	$3^3/4$	3.43	$5^3/4$	5.26	$7^3/4$	7.09	$9^3/4$	8.92
$1^7/8$	1.71	$3^7/8$	3.54	$5^7/8$	5.37	$7^7/8$	7.20	$9^7/8$	9.03
2	1.83	4	3.66	6	5.49	8	7.32	10	9.14

Index

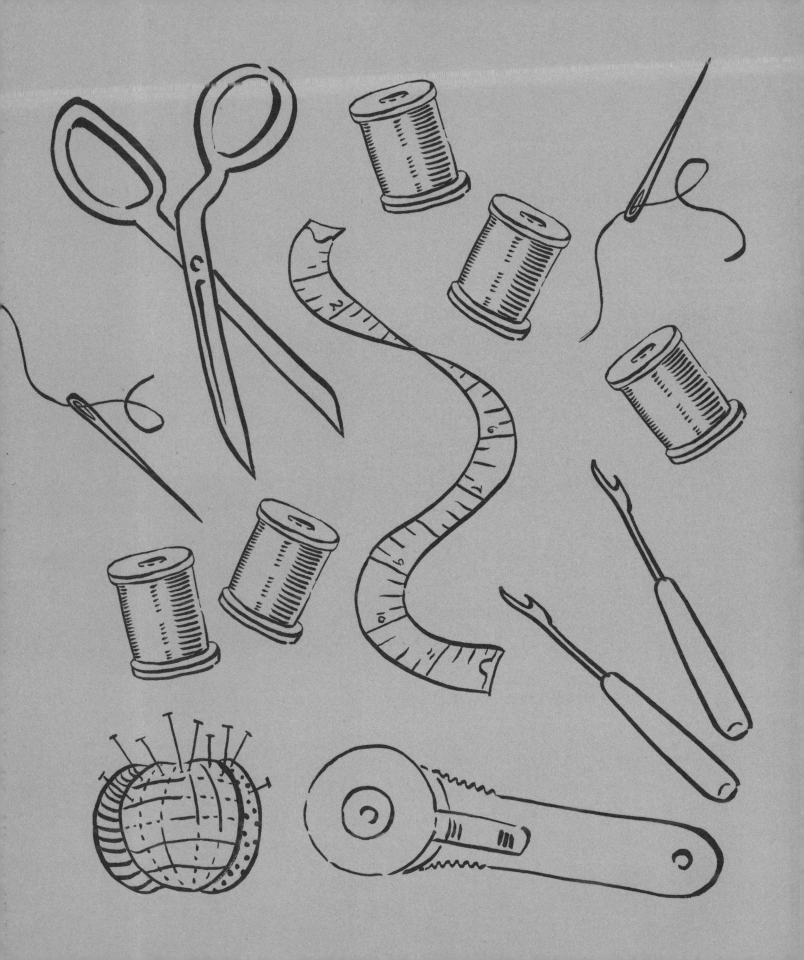